MY GRANDMOTHER'S KNITTING

FAMILY STORIES AND INSPIRED KNITS FROM TOP DESIGNERS

Larissa Brown

PHOTOGRAPHS BY MICHAEL CROUSER

STC CRAFT | A MELANIE FALICK BOOK

STEWART, TABORI & CHANG   NEW YORK

for OLIVE HOFKER

CONTENTS

WELCOME

My nanny, Olive.

MY GRANDMOTHER OLIVE'S NEW JERSEY SUMMER house was full of mysteries, from the ancient flowered bed sheets to the crocheted doll skirt that covered the toilet paper. It was a home straight out of 1959, and it never wavered as the decades passed. I thought it was magical—a place for family to gather, to while away time, read books, play games, slam screen doors, and eat lots of food, virtually all of it buttered.

It was also the place where I perpetrated my early knitting, always with Red Heart variegated acrylic yarn in vibrant colors against black. Nanny taught me the basic stitches, cast on for me, and then helped me through miles of scarves, which grew longer with every passing episode of *Days of Our Lives*. She was tough when it came to mistakes, peering through her cat's-eye glasses and stating, "We have to rip!" But she was also prone to laughter, happy to be spending time with me and making her specialty: crazy-colored afghans, many heavy with fringe. Eventually she helped me knit my first shaped objects, a pair of garter-stitch slippers. I still have her handwritten pattern for those slippers and the long aluminum needles we made them on, in metallic candy colors.

This book is like her summerhouse, full of memories, colors, textures, and surprises, with some playfulness, some wonder, and

some serious work getting done while everyone is enjoying themselves. Here, accomplished designers share their dearest memories of the people and places of their childhood that influenced their knitting. They also share twenty-two projects that are companions to these stories. Each design has an element that hearkens back to another time, yet is thoroughly contemporary and fun to knit.

The memories shared in this book are of grandmothers, called Gramma, Grams, Shorty, Nana. Of aunties and *tantes*. Of grandfathers, fathers, mothers. Many were knitters, but some were not. They were makers—if not of cardigans, then of violins, utility pole sculptures, or Japanese flower arrangements. They each had a profound impact on these designers' work. A kind of impact that you might recognize in your own family and your knitting today.

The stories in this book evoke details that welcome us into designers' family homes, as though we were right there wiping our feet on the doormat. We see the bright handknits in a cedar chest, hear the bug zapper, and feel the thunderstorm gusting through the screen porch. We step into Kay Gardiner's grandmother's clean, spare kitchen and can almost smell the pot roast, visit with Pam Allen's grandmother in the remote Ozarks and imagine we can feel her soft quilts under our hands. Kristin Spurkland takes us to the dramatic Alaskan landscape and invites us to touch the rough wool of Norwegian sweaters. Alongside their stories, designers share projects that I hope will become objects of fascination in your own house. A richly cabled Twining Vines Pillow or leafy Family Tree Afghan would be perfect for cuddling on an Adirondack chair on a chilly summer night, and a darling Grandma's Fan Dishcloth or two could grace the faucet of your gleaming sink.

Nanny and I didn't always choose the same colors, but we both loved a big pile of yarn.

For so many of us, there was a single person—a grandmother or grandfather, a family member, or perhaps a close family friend—whose spirit and style inspired us. Perhaps this book will remind you of someone remarkable who helped shape the knitter you are. The designers here consider their own special someones, and celebrate their humor, grace, fashion, creativity, and handiwork. Joan McGowan-Michael admires her mother's 1940s "wartime chic" style, and Jared Flood recognizes his father's stealth artistry building backyard sculptures. Wendy Bernard recalls fun times knitting on a Liberace-esque gold couch with her grandma, Helen. They made pom-pommed slippers that you can cast on for today, using the pattern she shares here.

Several designers reveal memories that go beyond one special person to whole families for whom it was normal to engage in everything from dressing up in grown-up clothes and performing original plays, to drawing masterpieces in crayon or knitting yards upon yards of I-cord. Their families surrounded them with the tools and materials to create whatever they could imagine. Their parents and grandparents were knitters, but also artists, mathematicians, inventors, hula dancers, and expert cookie bakers. They set a standard of creativity, and showed how a spark may be lit in the everyday.

Designer Kirsten Kapur tells us about her three great-aunts who could fashion anything they could imagine, from a needlepoint tour de force to a bottle-cap-embossed patio. Teva Durham and Norah Gaughan share stories of growing up with artist parents whose work infused their young lives. After reading about Teva's extraordinary grandmother Minerva, you may want to cast

I now treasure Olive's candy-colored needles.

on a slouchy bonnet named after her. Likewise, hearing about Leigh Radford's Auntie Edna, you may want to knit up her colorful namesake hat, or perhaps a few of them to distribute like holiday candy.

In fact, many of the stories here are about giving. They celebrate not only what we remember, but what we pass along to others now. Some of the projects make perfect gifts—a lacy Crocus Patch Baby Blanket, destined to become an heirloom, or a pair of precious Conover Mittens for a lucky child. In these pages, you'll find projects just right for teaching. You can walk a beginner through the process of creating a lovely, airy Storm Cloud Shawlette or a bold Crayon Cowl, both simple patterns with big impact. Even if you're not somebody's grandma, you have the chance to pass along your passion and skill, along with a love of texture and color, the thrill of a new idea, the confidence to try anything, and the satisfaction of a job well done.

Throughout our knitting world, there lurks the refrain "it's not your grandmother's knitting," meant to imply that our grandmothers were unsophisticated knitters, had outmoded ideas, lacked style, or were otherwise dowdy or uncool. This sentiment deprives us from really seeing knitting through our grandmothers' eyes and understanding what they loved about it. It discounts our grandparents' skill—in many cases developed over an entire lifetime—and also their style, individuality, and grace.

I hope this book will convince you—or just remind you—that the knitting we do *is* our grandmothers' knitting. Not only are the knits, purls, cables, and eyelets the same stitches our grandmothers made, but also the unique "knitter's hand" that comes through

The slipper instructions Olive wrote out for me when I was first learning to knit, and a pair of her long metal needles.

in each of our works is influenced in some part by the people we grew up with. (Personally, I live with a maddening habit of tugging my yarn after every stitch, the vestige of my Nanny's idiosyncrasy. But I inherited her daring color sense, too.)

I'm sure you have family memories as vivid as the ones retold on these pages. When I close my eyes, I can see Nanny and her summerhouse so clearly, from the big mimosa tree that we climbed and the pebbly front yard to the fringed blankets on the pull-out couch. I can hear her voice telling me how to move my hands to form purls or eyelets, or exclaiming that I'll "ruin my eyes" with the dark-colored yarn I preferred. And I can see her hands—lined like mine are becoming now—holding her cool metal needles.

Close your eyes. Tell me, who do you see?

One of Nanny's many multicolored afghans.

Family Stories

KNITTING AMONG THE NUDES

Wendy Bernard

W HEN WENDY BERNARD WAS A LITTLE GIRL, her grandma Helen would make her liverwurst or ham sandwiches for lunch. She and Wendy would sit and eat while Helen knit slippers with pom-poms.

Among the nudes.

Helen's husband was a sculptor of kitschy statues featuring naked ladies and cheeky captions. Young Wendy and her grandma hung out in their house and pondered the wonders of knitted afghans and slippers among busty girls arching their backs, their images captured in sculptures with taglines like "Ho Hum."

Decades later, Wendy is a well-loved knitwear designer and author known for her wit, charm, and flattering garments. She's written the *Custom Knits* book series and posts regularly on her spirited blog, Knit and Tonic. All this grew from Helen teaching her to knit, and from knitting together in her vibrant house.

Herman, the sculptor, called Helen "Shorty," and he claimed all the nudes were modeled after her. Nonetheless, she didn't allow them in the living room, her domain and sanctuary. The living room had heavy gold drapes—"very Liberace-esque"—and everything matched. A chandelier hangs twinkling in Wendy's memory. "She lived the good life," she says.

In their retirement years, Shorty and Herman celebrated happy hour every day. At 4:30 each afternoon, a BAR OPEN light would blink on. At 7:00 it would go off, and everyone would dump out their remaining drinks and trash their Spanish peanuts.

Shorty was super-fun, but sentimental, too, and a great keeper of beloved things. Wendy cross-stitched her some hand towels at age twelve, and they were still in Shorty's bathroom decades later. "I can't believe how well she took care of them. It was as if they hung in time, strange and magical," Wendy remembers. She had a pair of very clean couches, which remain a pristine gold to this day.

And she was an ordinary knitter of garden-variety blankets and slippers imbued with love. "Our generation does stunt knitting," Wendy declares. Her grandma never was a stunt knitter, but everyone went crazy for her simple slippers. At every holiday, they were the expected, coveted gift.

When Wendy was eight, Shorty showed her how to knit, purl, cast on, and bind off. Shorty also taught Wendy to knit for pure enjoyment—to relax, have fun, and make simple things people like, with family all around.

Happy hour with Herman and Shorty.

Memories of happy hours and even happier knitting are tinged with sad moments as well. Wendy visited Shorty when she was aging and rapidly losing her sight and memory. There were tremendous, sad events going on in everyone's lives, and the trip became lethargic and jumbled. Shorty wanted to knit, but, Wendy says, "She didn't recognize me, and we just didn't get to it. Grandma just touched the yarn and the needles. I remember her touching them."

Sometimes Wendy wishes for that moment back. Now in her nineties, Shorty no longer remembers how to knit. Wendy posits that may be why she herself knits and designs so much. "My knitting is so wrapped up in her," Wendy says, noting that making things for family and friends was always important. "She did a lot for me. I do that for my daughter now . . . and for other people."

Today, pure fun peeks out of all of Wendy's work. She calls her designs a bit "sexier and more carefree" than traditional hand-knits, and her blog nearly explodes with the love of spending time with family and good times. It seems Shorty taught her the basics quite well: Fun is life, giving is good, and being together is the most important thing. ✂

"Our generation does stunt knitting," Wendy declares. Her grandma never was a stunt knitter, but everyone went crazy for her simple slippers. At every holiday, they were the expected, coveted gift.

Cast on for slippers that could have been knit in Helen's living room. Wendy offers two versions, a "garden-variety" classic with pom-poms and a "stunt" version with flowers, on page 125.

BERTHA'S QUILTS

Pam Allen

P AM ALLEN HAS TAUGHT THOUSANDS OF PEOPLE—
maybe tens of thousands—to knit, through her
book *Knitting for Dummies*. She is a well-loved and
respected designer and author, the former editor of
Interweave Knits magazine, and the former creative
director of Classic Elite Yarns.

Today, Pam is the co-owner of Quince & Co., producing yarn in
a historic mill in Biddeford, Maine. Once a maker of horse twine,
the mill now spins Pam's signature yarns, which are sourced primarily in the United States with fiber from Merino, Rambouillet,
and Columbia-based sheep that roam the ranges of Montana
and Wyoming. Appreciating the history that is inherent in that
mill is a point of view she may have inherited in no small part
from her maternal grandmother, Bertha McRill. Grandma Bertha's
appreciation of the past manifested itself in scrappy keepsake
quilts made of used materials, each with its own story.

Bertha lived in Missouri in the remote Ozarks, and every summer Pam would leave her home in Chicago to visit that very different place. Bertha was full of easy creativity, with a strong sense
of self and a home life that was intensely memorable to little Pam.

"Her hair was down to her waist, and she washed it with Tide
detergent," Pam says, the sentence itself an invitation to step
onto her grandmother's porch. With great affection, she describes
Bertha's small home with creaky floors and a wringer washing

machine. "I loved to help her crank and squeeze the water out," Pam says. There were canned peaches in the basement, and Bertha made frog's-eye gravy with grease from the morning's bacon. Pam recalls a cool back porch. "When it rained, it sounded so good to sleep out there."

And within the enchantment of that summery house, there were quilts. Bertha was not a knitter, but her quilts were awesome to Pam, full of wonder. By the time Pam got her hands on them, some were already hard-used and fraying. Pam was shown how to handle them with reverence and care. "It was a big deal to take out the wedding ring quilt," Pam remembers. As a child who only got these special glimpses of the quilts, Pam was spellbound.

Bertha's quilts were made of pieces of clothing, linens, curtains—fabrics that told stories about other places and times. "You could point to any square and talk about where it came from," Pam says. "My mother could look at each one and say, 'First day of school, fifth grade.' Whole wardrobes and histories were recorded in those quilts. It was really magic to me."

It's not surprising, then, that Pam loves piecing together odd yards and colors and textures of yarn that hold stories and stray thoughts and intentions—the oddballs so many people might throw away. "I have an affinity for leftovers," she says.

In fact, she made her first original design in 1989—a square-necked vest with a Fair Isle design—out of leftover yarn. Today, even after a long career at the forefront of the knitting industry, she still loves the simple, creative challenge of a bag of yarn scraps that can make her see with new eyes. "You see surprising things, things you don't see until the yarns are lying together."

About this photo of Bertha, Pam says, "Anyone who knows me will tell you that the stance and hand gesture are genetic. She looks like me (or vice versa)."

Pam enjoys incorporating scraps willy-nilly. Everything changes when it touches something unexpected.

She inherited this sensibility from her grandma, for whom a quilt was something satisfying and beautiful made by juxtaposing leftovers—a way to save moments in time by plucking memories from the scrap bin. Pam calls it "saving pieces of history," and one cannot help but connect this phrase with the new yarn she now creates in Maine, every skein steeped in the history of that New England mill. It's an inspiration Pam absorbed from so many girlhood summer afternoons spent ghosting her fingers over quilt squares and whispering places and names and dates. It propelled her into a career that has evolved from knitter to designer, author, teacher, editor . . . and now creator of yarn. ✄

Pam's lavishly cabled Chickadee Cowl on page 127 is worked in wool spun in a historic Maine mill that Pam helped rescue from disuse.

Bertha's quilts were made of pieces of clothing, linens, curtains—fabrics that told stories about other places and times. "You could point to any square and talk about where it came from," Pam says.

EZ: NO SUCH THING AS WRONG

Meg Swansen

"**M**Y MOTHER WAS KNITTING ON THE PORCH THAT overlooked the river," says Meg Swansen, recalling her first knitting lesson when she was about five years old. "I stood in front of her, and she reached her arms around me to hold and guide my hands through my first stitches."

It is a tender moment that has been played out in countless homes, on a thousand riverbanks, and in a million different ways. But Meg's mother—Elizabeth Zimmermann—wasn't your average knitter, but perhaps the most well loved, respected, and famously opinionated knitter in the modern history of the craft.

EZ, as knitters affectionately call her, was born in outside London, in Maida Vale, in 1910. She immigrated to the United States around World War II, and by the late 1950s was starting to revolutionize the craft. From the family's large house in Shorewood, Wisconsin, Elizabeth began a mail-order yarn business and launched a newsletter called *Wool Gathering*, both of which Meg continues to run to this day.

EZ's work was always fresh and inventive, but not whimsical. She wrote patterns in plain language and based her innovations on common sense and math. She convinced generations of knitters of the merits of knitting in the round and devised EPS (Elizabeth's Percentage System)—a mathematical formula for fitting and shaping a sweater based, quite logically, on the

Little Meg's first completed project—a garter-stitch scarf for her Auntie Pete—revealed EZ's touch in the advanced and very practical use of short rows to shape the neck.

proportions of the human body. She introduced knitters to the elegantly simple I-cord, and a fundamental shawl formula based on the number pi.

She also had a wicked sense of humor. She wrote four books, all classics, including *Knitting Without Tears* and *Knitter's Almanac*. Her writing style was direct, personal, and conversational. A series of autobiographical essays called "Digressions"—in her book *Knitting Around*—were written for her children but introduced knitters everywhere to her dry wit and straightforward spirit.

Little Meg's first completed project—a garter-stitch scarf for her Auntie Pete—revealed EZ's touch in the advanced and very practical use of short rows to shape the neck. Knitting stayed with Meg for the next three decades, through school, travel, and adventure. A stint as a ski bum inspired her to knit a few of her mother's sweater designs. Her marriage to musician Chris Swansen in 1964 led to a move to Manhattan, where she knit sweaters for jazz musicians like Stan Getz and Gary Burton, sold her own designs to *Woman's Day*, and started acting as the "eastern branch" of Elizabeth's mail-order business.

Their business partnership was cemented when Meg and Chris, with two small children, joined Elizabeth in Wisconsin, where mother and daughter became a designing, writing, teaching, and publishing duo until Elizabeth's retirement in 1990. Today Meg lives in a converted schoolhouse on Cary Bluff in Pittsville, continuing the work of her family's Schoolhouse Press. She currently publishes knitting books, writes the semiannual *Wool Gathering* newsletter, produces instructional videos, designs for major knitting magazines, and writes a column for *Vogue Knitting*.

Elizabeth taught Meg to knit when she was about five years old.

Meg's mother was not the only creative force in her family. "All the women in my mother's family knitted—as did most British girls and women," she says, although being first-generation American meant that she never met most of those relatives. "My father was a linguist, a fly fisherman, author of several children's books—and a brewmaster by trade." Her father's family was from Germany, and well known in the European art world. Her grandfather, Walter Zimmermann, was curator of Munich's Glaspalast Exhibition Hall. His grandfather was the famous painter Ernst Zimmermann, and his great-grandfather "an even more famous painter," Reinhard Sebastian Zimmermann, whose works hang in the Alte Pinakothek museum, also in Munich.

But while Meg came from a long line of creative people, Elizabeth was her closest creative inspiration and guide. Growing up with her powerful influence, Meg inherited a good deal of her knitting values and beliefs.

"In my mother's knitting books is embedded a philosophy that tends to spill over into the rest of one's life: You are in charge of your own knitting; there is no such thing as 'wrong.' If you are pleased with the result, you are doing it 'right,'" Meg says, then adds, "not that there isn't always room for improvement." Lifelong learning and invention and innovation—traits she shared with her mother—are built in to the very fabric of her work.

"Knitting is power and can be a fulfilling means of self-expression, with a useful and lovingly made garment as a side bonus." Elizabeth taught her it is also "rather subversive." She says, "How many things are there in your life over which you have total control?"

EZ on the steps of the back porch in New Hope, Pennsylvania, where Meg's lifetime love of knitting began.

One way that Meg passes this idea along is through Knitting Camp, which was established in 1974, having evolved from a class Elizabeth taught at an extension of the University of Wisconsin. Nearly forty years later, getting into one of three Knitting Camp sessions held each summer is like scoring tickets to a sold-out rock concert.

Knitting Camp attendee Jenna Adorno wrote of her camp experience in the online magazine *Knitty*: "You can even practice your Kitchener stitch join on the tiny gauge swatches that Elizabeth created thirty years ago. Meg will put them in your hand with a darning needle, and you will feel like part of her family."

That invitation to step inside, pick up the needles and swatches, and become like family permeates all of Elizabeth's work. Meg mused about her mother in an interview published on the Knitting Universe website, after her death in 1999: "To read her is to know her, because there was no difference between the way she spoke and the way she wrote letters, or the way she wrote books."

Perhaps that is what makes Elizabeth feel like family for so many of us, even though we will never meet. Her books, Knitting Camp, and newsletters all make us feel like we belong. We can almost feel what it would be like to learn, as Meg did, on a porch by a river, surrounded by the arms of experience, looking out on an ever-flowing stream of possibilities. ✄

"In my mother's knitting books is embedded a philosophy that tends to spill over into the rest of one's life: You are in charge of your own knitting; there is no such thing as 'wrong.' If you are pleased with the result, you are doing it 'right.'"

DOESN'T *YOUR* GRANDPA KNIT?

Ysolda Teague

YSOLDA TEAGUE'S GRANDFATHER, WILLIAM STEWART, was a man who appreciated process. He lovingly made things he could not use. He handcrafted violins, but was tone deaf and could not play. He knitted items he himself would never wear, including sweaters for little Ysolda, growing up in Scotland in the early 1990s.

"When I went to nursery, I remember arguing that the other kids were all wrong," Ysolda says, "because their jumpers were knitted by their grannies."

Her grandfather is a romantic figure in her memory, an epicure of creativity who could move fluidly from knitting and making instruments to growing an abundant, green garden or doing punch-card programming for the paper mill where he worked. William was not bound by typical ways of seeing. Creativity and math were intertwined for him, just as they are for Ysolda, who is now a well-known knitwear designer. Her work showcases repetitive and geometric patterns, from the contours of a shoulder-hugging shawl to the ever-decreasing whorls of her signature tams. The knitter's and mathematician's brains work similarly, she says, both adept at seeing patterns.

Ysolda came to her career as a designer almost accidentally. "I couldn't really afford to buy patterns," she says, and making them up for herself, she noticed better ways to shape garments and execute techniques and began writing down her own inventive

Ysolda and William, her grandfather.

solutions. She posted pictures of her work on the Internet and was flooded with requests for instructions, so she began submitting patterns for publication. At the age of twenty, she saw her first pattern debut in *Knitty* magazine online.

Ysolda soon learned that some designers self-publish and sell their own patterns online, and she followed that model, using the Internet to very quickly transition from English literature student to worldwide knitting sensation. She now has thousands of daily visitors to her blog, which is simply called Ysolda, and a big community of fans on Ravelry, the popular Internet knitting community. Her patterns are available at online venues like *Knitty* and Twist Collective, and she self-publishes books that are available through her website. Knitters are mad for her designs; when she releases a new pattern, thousands of copies sell in a single day.

Considering Ysolda's first attempts at knitting, this kind of career seems unlikely. She was around six years old when she begged her mother to teach her, then got frustrated. "I wanted to knit lace doll clothes, not a garter-stitch rectangle. I didn't want her to touch my needles. They were *my* needles. I didn't want her to fix my mistakes. They were *my* mistakes." Ysolda laughs now. "I think it involved a lot of arguing and not much knitting."

Yet at age six, she already had the makings of a knitter who would one day turn the patterns she tried to follow on their heads, reimagining the way they worked, finding new, better ways to create the shapes and silhouettes she desired. "I'm not one to follow directions," she says.

She speaks admiringly of her aunt Catherine, who, at age ten, dove into knitting a complex Aran sweater because she wanted one

Looking back, it seems to Ysolda that everyone in her family knew how to knit. Yet her grandfather's practice of the craft stands out in her memory, like a snapshot of a simple scene. "I remember hanging out with him and playing while he worked. I liked to hold the yarn when he wound it."

for a school trip, and "no one told her she couldn't." As Ysolda developed as a self-taught seamstress and knitter, she collected needlework books from the 1940s. "I liked the attitude in those books, that you can just do things yourself." That attitude is a thread running through everything Ysolda designs. She's known for unexpected shaping as well as the whimsy of glossy ribbons, and pretty pale blues overlaid with brilliant red.

Looking back, it seems to Ysolda that everyone in her family knew how to knit. Yet her grandfather's practice of the craft stands out in her memory, like a snapshot of a simple scene. "I remember hanging out with him and playing while he worked. I liked to hold the yarn when he wound it."

She absorbed important lessons from him and from other family members, like her aunt Catherine, whose bold creativity made them kindred spirits: You can immerse yourself in making things, enjoying the puzzle and the math and the process, and not knit simply to have a mitten or a hat. You can create things with your own hands, your own way, using your intelligence as your guide. You can forge ahead with knitting and creativity and never let can't or shouldn't hold you back.

Her shawls, tams, sweaters, and stuffed toys are fanciful and imaginative, with a good dose of adventure and an eye for texture and pattern. Ysolda creates fairy-tale projects with names like Rapunzel and Gretel, and like those heroines, their sweetness is touched with something bold. Each pattern at first seems to be a precious flower, until one realizes it's tucked into the blond hair of a sassy little girl who refused to start with garter stitch. ✄

Ysolda's pattern for fingerless Fiddler's Mitts appears on page 95. She named them in honor of one of William's favorite crafts, making violins.

A QUARTER MILLION GRANNIES

Jessica Marshall Forbes

J ESSICA MARSHALL FORBES HAS PERHAPS A QUARTER-million "grannies" thanks to a website she founded called Ravelry. Together with her husband, Casey, Jess invented the site in 2007. It immediately started drawing knitters, crocheters, designers, spinners, and all manner of fiber enthusiasts like a million eager moths.

Naturally, many of those members are grandmothers, aunties, mothers, fathers, and grandpas who have joined Ravelry to share their thoughts and projects. And just as happens at yarn shops around the world, deep relationships have formed. A lot of otherwise unrelated members now feel like family, even if they've only met online.

Ravelry goes far beyond the typical Internet forum model, where people chat about a common interest. Knitters use Ravelry to track their stashes, plan and share projects and experiences, connect and inspire one another, and show off their skills. It is, perhaps, the highest-functioning relational database out there, cross-linking hundreds of thousands of projects with the yarns used, pattern sources, and knitters' chatter. It is likely because of this combination of utility, fun, and community that the site is steadily growing and has members hailing from nearly every corner of the globe. (A fascinating statistics page shows a world map of members currently online.)

Ravelry is the logical outcome of a yarn obsession that had a very humble beginning when Jess was around thirteen years old, and her grandma Fran taught her the basic knitting skills. Jess doesn't remember the moment, but a bit of sleuthing turned up a photo of them knitting together in Jess's rural New Jersey home. "Since then, we've found blobs that I made, shoved in the attic," she says.

After her short stint in blob-making, Jess "kind of gave up knitting" and picked up other crafts, especially enjoying complex, beaded cross-stitch projects. As an adult living in Cambridge, Massachusetts, and riding a commuter rail train to work, Jess realized her huge embroidery canvases and tiny beads were "not exactly portable," but knitting was. She bought *Knitting for Dummies*, by Pam Allen (see page 15), and set out to renew everything she'd learned from her grandma. Although her first project was "a hat that is too big for any human head," knitting stuck this time.

Soon, Jess entered the world of knitting bloggers who were storming the Internet in the early 2000s, looking to one another for ideas, inspiration, and cautionary tales. Jess waded daily into the ocean of communication available from fiber lovers, but became frustrated when the particular information she sought—the real gems of personal knitting stories, or specifics on a yarn or pattern she was considering—kept getting harder to find. Her husband, Casey, who worked as a computer programmer, suspected he could help by building a website that would solve these knitterly problems. In early 2007, they began work on the venture, and by that summer the tremendous response from hundreds of thousands of users—who not only flocked to get accounts but also

Jess, her mom Judy, and her Grandma Fran, who was a knitter and quilter.

donated money and bought Ravelry swag—allowed them to quit their day jobs and work on Ravelry full-time.

Now the site is home to hundreds of groups of knitters with common interests. Many of these groups—with names like Grandma's Hands, Crafty Aunties, and Large Families Unite!—celebrate deeply rooted relationships among family members. A Knitting Genealogists group has more than five hundred members. Our Ravelry Family is for those who have grandparents, parents, children, spouses, and other relatives who are also members of the site. "There are a lot of mothers and daughters," Jess says. "Some are young children or teenagers, who make groups and friends, and whose parents have accounts so they can also be involved." And for every young knitter, Jess sees ten more who are grandmothers, including people eighty and older.

"It's multigenerational," she says. "It's so great to see people of all ages talking about knitting and sharing ideas. It's happening all day and night. It's always there."

No one is in a better position than Jess to understand how knitting brings people together, and how dramatically different knitters can become like family. It's a phenomenon as old as sticks and string. And now thanks to Jess and Casey, it's possible for kindred knitting spirits to find each other, and to knit together, even if they live thousands of miles apart. ✂

About Ravelry, Jess says, "It's multigenerational. It's great to see people of all ages talking about knitting and sharing ideas. It's happening all day and night. It's always there."

SIMPLE IS COZY

Kay Gardiner

MABEL GARDINER WAS A CLEAR-EYED DANISH woman born of immigrant parents, who felt no nostalgia for the hard farm life of her childhood. But when her granddaughter—author Kay Gardiner, half of the well-known Mason-Dixon Knitting team—knew her in the 1970s, "everything was joyful in her life." When Kay was in elementary school in Omaha, Nebraska, Mabel was a bread-baking, doting grandmother who shared not store-bought treats, but time. She gave Kay a place of contentment at her kitchen table—a place of stainless steel, pot roast aromas, and Depression-glass green. Mabel was rigorous in a way her granddaughter speaks of with admiration and deep love. "She didn't need Tupperware," Kay marvels. "She unerringly made the exact amount of food needed."

Together with Ann Shayne, Kay has created the Mason-Dixon Knitting blog and two related books. Laughter and humor are woven through every one of her essays about knitting. As a designer, Kay is known for using fundamental knitting shapes, like afghan squares, as canvases for wild colors and creative approaches. She's also known for her love of dishcloths—in particular a dishcloth design with a bricklike construction within which she can play with an infinite palette. Kay has patience for the classics, and renders them in shiny, new color schemes. She'll sit and tend a field of simple garter stitch until it becomes stunning in its volume and grace.

She inherited much of her spare, inventive approach from her grandparents. Kay remembers their home vividly as a stripped-back, neat place where it was perpetually 1937. "The sofa was the sofa," she says. "It didn't change in thirty years." There was no need for an abundance of stuff, nor for frilliness. No cute tea towel adorned the faucet of the big, shiny sink. Her grandparents had a "habit of frugality" that has left the grown-up Kay with a love of the unfussy. "I think simple is cozy," she says.

While Kay's grandmother commanded inside the house, her grandpa Frank owned the outside, a place of green and stony wonder. A retired stone mason and a gardener, "his default position was making something with his hands," Kay says. He made the stone wall Kay would jump over to get from her house to theirs. He made the most beautiful garbage can enclosure in town. Kay helped him tend a half-acre garden, and together they hauled water across the street to the plot.

Today, Kay's knitting, designing, and writing are like an off-shoot from that garden—an inheritance of her family's gift for creating simple, well-made items.

Kay feels all the nostalgia her grandmother never did. She speaks with love about her time with her grandparents. She admired them, and one can see the impact they've had on her work. Their spirits come through in Kay's well-turned log cabin blankets, classic yet wildly angled quilts, and simple signature dishcloths, their squares stacked like stones in a pretty cotton wall. ✄

Kay's grandmother Mabel was a constant presence during Kay's childhood.

ANGELINA AND HER SISTERS

Joan McGowan-Michael

"MY MOTHER WAS A 1940S FASHIONISTA," SAYS Joan McGowan-Michael, with clear love and admiration. It was, Joan says, "no mean feat during wartime," with rationing of supplies and scarce income. It took ingenuity and a strong creative will—two things her mom had in abundance.

Seventy years later, Joan herself is the go-to expert on hand-knitting designs for inventive, retro-inspired garments, with a focus on 1940s-style lingerie. Every day, she delivers to thousands of knitters the blueprints for beautiful works of art that flatter the range of feminine forms. Her design specialty seems apropos, given the easy style, creativity, and grace Joan speaks of when she recalls her mom's teen and young adult years living on Alabama Street in San Francisco.

"With their husbands away at war, she and her three sisters lived at home but held full-time jobs as secretaries or hairdressers," Joan explains. Not having a lot of money to spend on clothes, Joan's mother, Angela—called by the diminutive Angelina—would cut up old clothing and make her own incredible wardrobe. "My grandfather had a lot of really good suits," Joan says. "Many of the things my mother wore were made of them."

And what she wore was fabulous. A cascade of black-and-white family photos shows Joan's mother and her sisters in one innovative, handcrafted outfit after another, accessorized with

Not having a lot of money to spend on clothes, Joan's mother, Angelina, would cut up old clothing and make her own incredible wardrobe.

gorgeous little handbags and shoes, chic hats, and furs flung over their shoulders. They weren't wealthy. They were ingenious. They reused, remixed, shared, and swapped pieces so it seemed that each of them always had the latest fashions.

Joan was impressed by these photos, and she absorbed her mother's casual glamour and sense of fashion adventure like only a child can. She grew up to study and train as a fashion designer, and her first design job, in the 1980s, was for the lingerie superpower Frederick's of Hollywood. "There were no actual seasons to design for per se, and vulgar was the order of the day!" Joan exclaims. "But at the end of the day, the things had to fit, and that was where I got my first real dose of working a garment until it fit the widest range of people possible."

It was thanks to her mother that Joan pursued a career in hand knitting. Angelina was "a very big knitter" who taught Joan to cast on and knit when she was a girl. "I really remember wanting to know how," Joan says. "I saw someone on TV, and it looked like the lady was rubbing sticks together and fabric was appearing." So when she happened upon her mom's old knitting bag in her closet, Joan demanded to be taught. After she learned the basics from her mother, she continued her knitting education using Girl Scout handbooks from the library.

She was engrossed. "I was knitting and crocheting myself accessories as an eight-year-old, and sewing my own versions of the current fashions at twelve." Her mother supported her implicitly. "Though we weren't a financially well-off family, it was understood that if I wanted fabric or yarn to make things with, all I needed to do was ask."

Joan's stylish mother, Angelina.

Her mother's creativity was amazing, but not everything Angelina made was entirely graceful. In fact, one infamous project her mother knit taught Joan a lesson in what not to do. "In the 1960s, Mom was working on a little sweater," she says. "She miscounted and had too many stitches on the needles, and judging by the finished product, I can tell she just decided to decrease all on one row." The result was a tight gathering effect—right smack across the bust. "When she would wear this sweater, she would carry her purse or something over her chest," Joan laughs. "It took a heck of a lot of energy to hide the mistake. In a roundabout way, she taught me to have some patience and do things right the first time."

In Joan's memory, that sweater seems an isolated error of enthusiasm, made by a woman who was blessed with a natural talent and daring spirit for pulling together disparate pieces and making just the clothes she wanted. Joan is fascinated and moved by her mother's—and aunts'—styles. "I am positive that seeing the photos and home movies of them was one of the biggest influences on my own design aesthetic," she writes on her blog, White Lies Knits.

Like much of the war-era women's fashion, Joan's work brings together sensible shaping and enduring elegance. Her designs are known throughout the knitting world for their big collars, flattering slim waists, and sweeping romanticism. Vintage chic circa 1944 is in Joan's blood. "I can't imagine ever getting tired of it," she says.

In 2001, Joan founded her company, White Lies Designs, to share this design vision, specializing in patterns for lacy, lush women's garments that fit a range of women's sizes, from 34-inch to 64-inch busts. In 2007, her book *Knitting Lingerie Style* captured her distinctive style.

And it made her mother sublimely proud. Angela was in her eighties and growing increasingly ill by the time Joan was able to put a published copy in her hands. She read it silently. "When she came to the end, she closed it carefully and told me how proud of me she was and how seeing this completed was one of the high points of her life," Joan says. "Her death was the single most difficult thing I've ever lived through, but it soothes some of that pain in my heart to know I made her so proud."

Joan is fascinated and moved by her mother's—and aunts'—styles. "I am positive that seeing the photos and home movies of them was one of the biggest influences on my own design aesthetic."

Joan shares a pattern for a fabulous 1940s-style shrug on page 85.

TRUE RED

Kristin Spurkland

KRISTIN SPURKLAND'S FATHER, TORBJØRN SPURK-land, has a deep voice with a thick Norwegian accent, perfect for the stories that rolled off his tongue when little Kristin visited him in Alaska every summer growing up. They were stories of trolls turned to dramatic stone in the Alaskan landscape and of fairy-tale creatures living under leaves. She says of nature, "There's this unseen world going on in there," and she spreads her fingers over the table as if to draw that life up into her hands—and into her knitting.

As a knitwear designer and author of several books, including *Knits from the Heart* and *The Knitting Man(ual)*, Kristin is inspired by the landscape, the magic, and the Norwegian knitting traditions of her ancestors. She interprets traditional designs and silhouettes in new ways, and each sweater, blanket, or sock she creates is infused with something from her childhood, be it Norwegian culture or the colors and textures of the natural world.

Kristin grew up living with her mother, Ginny, in Oregon and Washington, but it is her dad's home in Alaska that she recalls in great, colorful detail. Outside, Tania, her stepmother, grew lush beds of Livingston daisies, a bright, deep orange sea still vivid in Kristin's mind today. The luscious, summery color complemented a more wintry treasure inside the house: a trunk full of equally vibrant Norwegian handknits.

Kristin's father, Torbjørn, or Tobben as he is known in America, in a sweater from his homeland, Norway.

Sweaters, socks, and hats virtually tumble out in Kristin's memory, in a heap that would enthrall many a colorwork fanatic. Her father's home was rather plain, but it was dotted with Nordic plates and knickknacks in his culture's traditional true red, and the chest of knitwear was an intense infusion of texture and beauty. Torbjørn learned to knit in school—everyone did in Norway—but he left knitting behind as he grew up. The really accomplished knitters in Kristin's family were her *tantes*, aunts who lived in Norway and were the source of many hats and sweaters she wore in her younger days. "They were steeked," she explains of the gift sweaters, "so they did this funny thing." She illustrates, raising her arms like a scarecrow. They were no doubt masterpieces, but Kristin found them a bit awkward—"none of my peers were wearing these."

Though Kristin eventually traveled to Norway several times and got to know her aunts, she did not grow up with needle arts. She learned to knit during her freshman year in college in the 1980s. An interest in New Wave music and culture, along with her knitting skills, eventually led to an apparel design degree.

Today her passion is applying a new palette to the traditional forms of her heritage. She dips into dusty pinks that are softer and less primary, sometimes bringing forward the fiery orange of her stepmother's daisies. She brings wilder or subtler colors to Nordic animal shapes, stars, and nature figures that are normally delivered in straightforward blues, reds, and creams. But no matter how far she ranges she always likes to keep a fillip of the simple, true red in her designs, the one that stood out among the knickknacks and plates in her father's home. ✄

Kristin applied her adventurous color sense to the Norwegian pullover pattern on page 99.

FASHION MOMENTS

Teva Durham

When Teva Durham speaks of her grandmother Minerva, it's with the adoration of an awed little girl. "She was theatrical," Teva says of her maternal grandmother, or "nani." "She had a booming voice. She made scenes." She is exceptional in Teva's memory, even among a family of creative makers—including parents who are artists and educators. Minerva invited Teva to be dramatic, creative, and free.

Teva is, in fact, known for those qualities. As a designer of sculptural garments and accessories, and as an editor at *Vogue Knitting* magazine, Teva was at the forefront of the wide resurgence of knitting beginning in the late 1990s. Her writing and designs are featured in magazines, compilation books, and her own series of *Loop-d-Loop* knitting and crochet books. Recently, she created a yarn line with the same name.

Her work combines established and historical knitting techniques and striking design elements, such as big stand-up collars and huge bell sleeves. She plays with scale and gauge, so that a single dropped stitch makes a striking ladder down the center of a vest, or one oversized leaf sets off the hemline of a whole pullover. She likens knitted pieces to theatrical characters. "I like them to speak," she says.

Like her designs, her signature yarns—created together with yarn company Tahki Stacy Charles—have drama built in. A brushed merino blend is made to give a unique felted effect when knitted. A bulky, lush wool roving is stitched down the center to create an unusual texture in big stitches.

Teva's eye for pleasing lines and shapes was nurtured by her parents. Her father ran the art department at a junior college, and her mother taught at Parsons School of Design. They did not teach her to draw formally, but whenever she showed an interest, they would set up still lifes or invite her to create self-portraits they would gently critique, and their guidance set her up for a future doing fashion sketches. "Being around creativity, you get it by osmosis. As a child, I got a sense of sketching from life and wanting to practice, document things, and express myself that way."

When Teva was in elementary school in St. Louis, her nani visited frequently. It was during one of those visits that she taught Teva to knit.

It was also during one of those visits that she exposed Teva to her first "fashion moment." Teva recalls, "Nani took me to Famous & Barr and bought me a camel-colored cashmere turtleneck, and I was in love with the feel of it." Minerva also bought her a Cowichan wrap sweater to go with it. "This was the seventies. At that time it was very sophisticated to have a belted sweater. To me, it was glamorous." Teva adds, "I also wanted the cool Frye boots. You had to beg to get them. They were, like, a hundred dollars."

Minerva eventually moved to St. Louis, where she helped Teva achieve more of her key "fashion moments," including the successful sewing of a prom dress on a black Singer treadle sewing machine with $75-a-yard eyelet fabric (a grandmother's indulgence). Teva recalls happily, "It was sort of *Saturday Night Fever*."

Teva's spectacular nani, Minerva.

Minerva brought a sense of adventure and individuality to her personal knitting, often making uncommon pieces that seem to be the ancestors of Teva's own design work. For example, she made original "bandeaus," which Teva explains were distinctive tube tops. Minerva was unafraid of huge, bulky stitches, and she regularly worked with two colors of Red Heart yarn held together.

Eventually, her nani helped launch Teva into her knitting career, though in a sadly roundabout way. When Minerva passed away, Teva, who was about twenty years old, learned that Nani had set aside some money to help her travel in Europe. She stayed in Paris for months, and that was when knitting became more than a hobby.

In Paris, she was exposed to the work of British designer Patricia Roberts, whom Teva says was "really hot" at the time, revolutionizing what people knit at home with her patterns and kits for wild and stylish garments. "Around that time, *Vogue Knitting* came out. It was bubble sweater time," she says in reference to a spectacularly oversized pullover by Marc Jacobs. Inspired by these designers and the energy of the knitting industry, Teva's own design work began to emerge.

That Parisian excitement is still present in her work. "Designing and this job—it's like being a kid again," Teva muses. "The fantasy of paper dolls or Barbie. At the same time, I take it very seriously. I have very high self-standards."

Now Teva has her own daughter, Olivia, eight, who seems to have bypassed the typical basic clothes and mangled hairdos that Barbies everywhere put up with. She recently worked on her own fall collection concurrently with Teva. Olivia drew a sketch—"done

Minerva was unafraid of huge, bulky stitches, and she regularly worked with two colors of Red Heart yarn held together.

freehand, no tracing"—of a slouchy, oversized sweater on a girl with a pouty face and big Goth hair. "I think she has been influenced by my work," Teva says proudly. "Look at the sweater yoke. And I love her color sense. I love that she accessorized with roller skates and an iPod."

Teva's father has said about teaching art to children, "It's best, I believe, to quietly open doors to a world of many possibilities." Her grandmother and parents clearly opened those doors for Teva, who is making sure they stay open for Olivia, too. ✂

Make Teva's interpretation of Minerva's favorite slouchy bonnet, the one she's wearing in the photo on page 37. Teva has updated its 1920s appeal in the pattern on page 103.

A STEALTH CREATIVE
Jared Flood

J ARED FLOOD'S FATHER BUILDS THINGS. Jared describes his dad, Jeff, as a "stealth creative," blue-collar worker who is also a natural and somewhat casual builder of amazing works of art crafted from telephone poles and salvaged industrial materials. When Jared speaks of these constructions, he shares a sense of himself as a little kid, not entirely sure if what his dad is doing is cool or not. But it's clear that as an adult he looks on Jeff's backyard creations with love and a grown-up respect. "He has a way of looking at discarded, distressed materials. He sees beauty in the unsightly. He's got an eye I hadn't appreciated when I was younger."

Jared's own work is far more public and widely known. He's a talented knitwear designer, photographer, author of the blog Brooklyn Tweed and the pattern collection Made in Brooklyn, and the creator of a yarn line called Shelter.

Jared grew up in a rambler house in suburban Washington, brimming with family, including his parents, himself, and two brothers. The backyard was his dad's creative playground—literally. "He built us this giant part-fireman-pole-part-treehouse," Jared recalls. As he describes a fantasia of wood and metal, the rough materials seem to be right under his fingertips.

Dad's art has few limits, but always a function. A playground or swimming pool or other useful structure is always the result. And he always uses rough-hewn, distressed, and often massive materials, such as railroad ties or utility poles. That combination of beauty, usefulness, and strong physical presence is what Jared appreciates most. "The things he builds are super-solid, not nebulous."

Jared's mom, Gail, enjoys more traditional creative pursuits; she's been a quilter for more than twenty years. Jared was so used to her hand-wrought works of art lying around the house that it took a formal art education at the New York Academy of Art for him to recognize the talent that was right in front of him. "After coming home from school for painting, I told her she was an incredible artist," Jared admits, laughing at his high compliment.

While it was his mother who initially taught him to knit at age six, Jared picked up the craft again while in college, not suspecting it would have such a profound effect on his life. "I was deep in the culture of art for art's sake," he says, but eventually, art without function lost its appeal. "I think part of it is that my parents have a function motivation for their creativity." Knitting fed his desire for combined beauty and utility. He taught himself to develop and refine his skills, and he became more and more involved with it. "I kept not *not* liking it," he says of the way the craft grew on him, almost under the radar.

A decade later, Jared is an accomplished designer and writer of a blog that is celebrated for its simple elegance and lush yet spare photography. His designs have been featured in *Vogue Knitting*, *Interweave Knits*, and several online venues, and he has designed and photographed pattern booklets for Classic Elite Yarns. He finds designing satisfying and challenging because it mixes working with his hands and the logic and math of writing a pattern.

Jared (in front), his dad, and his brothers, Ryan and Matt.

Dad's art had few limits, but always a function. A playground or swimming pool or other useful structure was always the result.

"You have the yarn and shape, and then you draw the map," he explains. He also finds knitting to be a perfect balance of art and utility. "Knitting," he says, reaching to touch a project that sits by his side, "is connected to your life. You're actually sharing a process with a person that turns out something good for them to use."

Jared's designs take simple, excellent yarn with rich surface detail and push it even further, texture-wise. An almost elemental Shetland wool or tweed is twined into cables that pop off the surface of a hat, scarf, or mittens. He says of texture, "I really feel like that's what my subject is."

One can see his dad's spirit and aesthetic when Jared repurposes a traditional shape. In his hands, a classic doily design—reimagined using much larger yarn and needles—becomes a gorgeous and useful afghan that will warm someone's lap. The geometric steel structure of the Seattle Public Library's iconic building is transformed into the interlocking cables of a warm wool hat. It's a way of seeing potential and beauty in everyday items that he credits to his dad, but which Jared himself has clearly inherited. As he talks about his father, he could easily be talking about himself. "He looks at things in a way that brings new meaning to them." ✂

Inspired by the architecture of an abandoned seaside military base, Jared designed the hat on page 105.

ART EVERYDAY

Norah Gaughan

NORAH GAUGHAN INVITES KNITTERS TO TRY OUT new ideas: knitting a skirt that resembles a turtle's shell, for example, or a sweater that begins at the center back and, as she describes it, "explodes outward in rings." Norah is inventive and fearless. She makes beautiful productions out of forms that occur in nature, and is known for creating brave new shapes and garments that are not only intriguing or wild, but also flattering and comfortable enough to become everyday favorites.

It's not surprising that Norah is the product of two artist parents and a home filled with invention and encouragement. Her mother, Phoebe, drew organic shapes and garden and craft illustrations for books and magazines. Her father, Jack, was one of the artists responsible for the distinctive 1960s style of science-fiction illustration, marked by line art and bold visions of the future.

Norah recalls many artistic experiences undertaken at her big, creative house. Her parents' friends, all artists, would visit and play games that tested and spurred Norah's imagination. The family dyed gorgeous Easter eggs, and her mother loved making elaborate Halloween costumes. One year, for their sci-fi-themed Halloween party, little Norah went as a gigantic papier mâché eyeball.

Their home in Rifton, New York, was a four-story stone structure that had once been a boarding house for the local carpet mill.

Jack, Norah's dad, helps her and her brother Brian put together a toy. Hanging behind them are two of Dad's science-fiction cover-art paintings.

It had big windows with deep sills and a sense of history. Her parents kept it like a live-in art salon, with hallways full of framed paintings and sketches.

When Norah was nine, her maternal grandmother, who lived with the Gaughans, taught her to crochet, and a few years later a family friend taught her to knit. Though her mother did not know how to use the needles, she was supportive and lovingly helped Norah through her first tearful sweater. Norah was a perfectionist and struggled with the sweater, resulting in what she calls "full-on crying jags." Her mom came across *Knitting Without Tears* by Elizabeth Zimmermann (see page 18) at the bookstore and knew it was just what Norah needed. "That book was the perfect thing for me," says Norah. "It led me to do what I wanted to do."

After inventing some original knitwear as a young teen, including some "weird vests," she had her first design published in 1979 in *Ladies Home Journal Needle & Craft*, while she was still in high school. In college at Brown University, she earned a dual degree in biology and art, subjects that informed her design style later on. Immediately after graduating, Norah answered an ad for a test knitter and began a long mentoring relationship with acclaimed designer Margery Winter, whose guidance and inspiration kept Norah moving in the direction of knitwear design.

Norah describes her post-college design work as "coming in big bursts of creativity." She later designed hundreds of stitch patterns, including intricate twists and cables, for commercial companies to use in garments. Today, she is the design director for Berroco—one of the largest yarn companies in the world. In that role, she leads a team in developing new yarns and color

Norah recalls many artistic experiences undertaken at her big, stony, creative house. Her parents' friends, all artists, would visit and play games that tested and spurred Norah's imagination.

palettes, and creating huge collections of projects that feature them. Her singular designs are featured in a series of Berroco pattern booklets.

Norah's dual interests in science and craft came together in her 2006 book *Knitting Nature*. It was a major work, inspired by *The Self-Made Tapestry: Pattern Formation in Nature,* by Philip Ball. For *Knitting Nature*, Norah designed projects based on six frequently occurring shapes, including the pentagon shape of a starfish, the spiral of a ram's horn, the phyllotaxis of a pinecone or cactus, and the movement and forms found in water.

Norah had the opportunity to work with her mother on *Knitting Nature*. Phoebe (whose Ravelry profile lists Norah herself as a work in progress) illustrated ogee and fractal shapes and a few simple diagrams. Her assessment of the final published book was her usual reaction to anything her daughter has created: "Oh, that's amazing!" She shows her support by regularly writing Norah letters that say things like, "You are way more creative than your father or I ever were."

This, Norah says, "is not really true."

Being raised with a sustained spirit of creative adventure and possibility, and the everyday expectation of art, had a lifelong impact. "Because of my family and who they were, I was set up to make whatever I wanted." ✂

MICHELINA'S AFGHANS

Anne Hanson

ANNE HANSON'S DESIGN CAREER—ONE THAT has inspired countless knitters to wrap loved ones in shawls, stoles, socks, and hats made with her lacy, light-filled patterns—has its origins in an afghan that lay draped over her mother's sofa when she was a little girl. It was an intricate sampler, knit by her mother's mother in the 1960s in shades of blue, with fifty different stitch patterns, from cables to lace.

Anne, who now designs from her home in Ohio, where she also writes her blog, Knitspot, was fascinated with that afghan at a very young age. "I used to lie there examining the surfaces for hours, feeling the stitches and holes, memorizing the traveling lines of the motifs, and making up stories in my head to go with them," she says. Anne was impressed that a person could make something like a blanket. "I wanted to do one myself."

At age three, she began pestering her grandma to teach her how to knit. "I would watch her and see the patterns coming off the needles, thinking I could figure it out." But a few early attempts proved that watching alone would not get her to the skill level she desired. So she waged a campaign to get Gram to show her.

Gram, also known as Michelina Nardolillo Bottari, always knitted. "If she was sitting, she was probably knitting," Anne says. "No reading, no puzzles, it was her one hobby." An Italian immigrant living in northern New York State, her grandmother was one of seven sisters—so many sisters, they had their own crochet club. They each paid dues, and the club took trips with the funds. "They worked hard for a living, and needlework was their relaxation," says Anne, who grew up believing that if she worked diligently around the house, knitting time would be her reward.

Anne figures Michelina made 100, perhaps even 150 afghans during her lifetime, including a gorgeous, sturdy wool blanket for each of her ten grandchildren. "I got mine when I was four years old," says Anne. "I still use it almost every night." After her grandchildren, Michelina knit for the rest of her huge Italian family of cousins, aunts, uncles, sisters. Someone was always getting married or having a baby, and Gram churned out wonderful blankets for all of them.

At age four, Anne finally got her wish, and Gram showed her the basic stitches. She recalls expecting to make cables on her first day. "I learned pretty quickly that knitting is hard," she says. But at age seven she successfully knit a pair of cabled mittens. By age twelve, Anne could sew a fully tailored suit, and she was designing knit and sewn garments in her teens. By age twenty, she could write her own knitting and sewing patterns.

Although she originally trained for a career in speech pathology, in the early 1980s Anne moved to New York City and decided to apply for work in the garment industry, "which appealed more to my inner life as a 'maker.'" With her home-honed skills, Anne became a stitcher, whose job it was to complete the finishing touches on a garment. Once she got a foothold in that industry, she began working in costuming, and moved her way up to being a pattern-maker/draper and eventually a designer sample room manager.

Anne (far left) with her grandparents and two of her siblings. On the back of the sofa is one of Gram's signature afghans.

"Stitch patterns fascinated her," Anne says of Gram, noting that she had a real facility for memorizing them and enjoyed the cadence and rhythm of repeating motifs. "I am the same," she observes. "I think that's the strongest way I identify with her as a knitter."

Undoubtedly, Michelina would have appreciated Anne's lace baby blanket pattern on page 109.

Throughout this time Anne never stopped knitting, and over the next twenty years, she continued with the craft, designing patterns for knitters as an increasing part of her work. She began publishing her blog, Knitspot, in 2006 and publishing her knitwear patterns online that same year.

Those patterns experiment with texture, light, space, and twisted stitches—all things that she first encountered in Gram's blankets. "Stitch patterns fascinated her," Anne says of Gram, noting that she had a real facility for memorizing them and enjoyed the cadence and rhythm of repeating motifs. "I am the same," she observes. "I think that's the strongest way I identify with her as a knitter." In fact, Anne's lace shawls and stoles—with names like Tudor Grace, Maplewing, and Ostrich Plumes—expand on stitch patterns that Gram probably knew well.

Throughout her career, Anne has relied on the simple lessons her grandmother's afghans represent. "We were exposed at a young age to all sorts of handwork, from carpentry to needlework, and taught to do these well and to be the best at them among our peers," she says of herself, her siblings, and her cousins. Less tangibly, and just as important, "I was taught from the very beginning to develop good instinct and an eye for beauty, balance, harmony, and good design."

Anne says, "My family made me confident about my work." She extends that confidence to the knitters she teaches, helping people create the works of art that will one day be heirlooms—as prized as Gram's fifty-pattern afghan that mesmerized her at age three. ✄

AUNTIE EDNA WAS LIKE FAMILY

Leigh Radford

L EIGH RADFORD SUBMITTED HER FIRST DESIGN proposal to *Interweave Knits* magazine in 2001. The editors asked, "What are you wearing?" Leigh recalls suddenly seeing Flaubert references everywhere she went, and she drew on memories of late-afternoon strolls through the flea market at Clignacourt to conjure up a sunset-hued sweater. She wrapped her swatches in a map of Paris to mail off to the editor.

It was the first step in a career in the knitting industry built upon a background in graphic arts and a lifetime of adventurous crafting. That first submission led, rather quickly, to her moving from Oregon to Colorado to be art director of *Interweave Knits*—a post she held for four years. Leigh was immersed in the craft. "I really got my feet wet, designing and learning from Ann Budd and others," she says. In addition to working on the magazine, Leigh contributed to Interweave Press's book department, consulting on book design and helping authors achieve their vision. But when Leigh became homesick for the Northwest—"I missed Portland and the water"—she left Colorado and returned home. Back in Portland, she wrote the well-loved books *AlterKnits* and *One Skein*, plus follow-up volumes to each.

Leigh's designs are daring and sure, ranging from knitted paper lanterns and mixed-media pillows to classic blankets and scarves that are simple but command attention for their scale, texture, and color. Her work blends felting, knitting, sewing, and a Japanese technique known as shibori, through which the knitter shapes and embellishes cloth by tying or binding it before felting or dyeing. One of her favorite creations is a stockinette-stitch screen door. She's unafraid to use materials and skills in unexpected ways.

That kind of artistic confidence and exploration comes naturally to Leigh, but was certainly nurtured by her "auntie" Edna—a friend of her grandmother Honey. "She was a schoolteacher. She played bridge with my grandmother," Leigh recalls of Edna in the late 1960s. "They were both quite stylish—always wearing hats and gloves and never seen without lipstick perfectly applied." She was like family, and she played a grandmotherly role in Leigh's crafting life, imparting the basic skills and some deeper lessons, too.

For starters, she showed Leigh that it was okay to knit. "At the time, women were being urged away from things that were deemed a little oppressive," says Leigh. But Edna was a strong example of someone who achieved a high skill level with her craft. "She was proficient," says Leigh. "She knit Chanel suits." She also knit playful hats for Leigh and her brother, Matt, to wear camping.

Auntie Edna taught Leigh to knit when she was around thirteen, and whenever she visited the small town of Albany, Oregon, where Leigh lived, she would show her something new. She watched as Leigh "bounced around from knitting and crocheting to sewing," and learned to work with leather and beads as a Bluebird—a young member of the Camp Fire organization. "I went through a macramé phase, too," Leigh recalls. Edna was always supportive, believing there are a lot of ways to creatively approach an idea.

Leigh—in a massive hair bow—and Matt, her brother, with their ever-stylish Auntie Edna.

Leigh learned from Edna "to choose the craft that does what you want and need." For example, Leigh says, "I like crocheting for its almost sculptural quality." It's the kind of thing Leigh hopes to inspire in other knitters as a writer and teacher. Her books *Alter-Knits* and *AlterKnits Felt* invite readers to go beyond a single craft and embrace a world of techniques and skills. *AlterKnits* includes creativity boosters that she likens to "warm-up exercises." They put the knitter into a state of mind where ideas can flow freely and confidently, and where a notion might slowly bloom—to alter, extend, or change something about a published pattern. She helps knitters make that leap, to become the kind of crafters who can adjust and bend patterns or materials to get a desired result.

These days, Leigh is working as an artist, and for the first time in years is not writing a knitting book. Instead, she's making a series of paintings for which she knitted her own canvases, and has just finished an installation of vessels knit of linen and filled with plaster. She uses her knitting the way Auntie Edna might have advised her to—as one skill among many, and as one ingredient in mixed-media works that expresses her artistic intent. ✄

Auntie Edna taught Leigh to knit when she was around thirteen, and whenever she visited the small town of Albany, Oregon, where Leigh lived, she would show her something new.

On page 117 Leigh offers a pattern for a playful hat like the ones that Edna used to make for her to wear during their annual camping trips.

AS GREEN IS TO A GARDEN

Chrissy Gardiner

MOST KIDS HAVE ONE HOME, ONE HOUSE, ONE yard to explore. Chrissy Gardiner had three—her parents', her grandmother's, and her aunt's—with yards and gardens to wander in, porches to sleep on during hot summer nights, and animals to feed. Each was a place where Chrissy, an only child, could immerse herself in nature and her own imagination, and where slowly her love of nature became entwined with fiber and craft.

Today she's an accomplished designer and author and the proprietor of Gardiner Yarn Works in Portland, Oregon. Her designs can be found in *Interweave Knits* magazine, in yarn company pattern lines, and in the collections of indie sock clubs, the kind that knitters join to receive exclusively dyed yarn and sock projects each month. She self-published her first book, *Toe Up!*, in 2009. But what really distinguishes her resume is the way her designs are steeped in the colors and forms of the natural world. Socks and shawls are covered in cables that recall twining vines and leaves. Textures bring to mind berries and seeds. The ruffle of a girlish sock mimics fresh lettuce in a sunny garden.

Her career had its roots in tiny Aitkin, Minnesota, where her parents raised her in a tidy and crisp house, all white winter sunlight and clotheslines in summer. "There was south and east exposure in the living room, so light was always streaming in," she says.

Outside there were two big cedars, a mini-orchard of crab apples, and her mother's big garden. The house was heated with wood and amazingly warm. At least one cat always sat on top of her dad's huge record collection.

If her parents' house was rich with life, then Grandma Artis's place was a riot. Chrissy's grandma Artis and grandpa Carl lived in Aitkin too, and their abode was a cozy, cluttered old farmhouse—"all angles," Chrissy says, illustrating the point with slashes of her hands. Artis and Carl raised dairy cows, and there were animals everywhere to touch and care for—chicks in a lighted cardboard box, calves that Chrissy fed with bottles.

One summer when Chrissy was about nine, she was exploring Grandma Artis's place and discovered a skein of Red Heart yarn and a pair of translucent knitting needles. "One had a metal end, and the other was broken and had a Battleship peg glued on," she recalls. Did her grandmother teach her to knit with those needles? Probably, Chrissy thinks, but the memories are hazy, and it seems there were several crafters in Chrissy's young world. There was a babysitter who taught her the thumb cast on to keep her occupied, and a great-aunt who showed her some stitches that have since become second nature. And then there was Aunt Marsha.

Aunt Marsha lived on an acre of verdant land in Munising, Michigan, a little town on the south shore of Lake Superior. Chrissy vacationed there for weeks each summer, walking and playing along grassy paths awash in green. Inside, Aunt Marsha had a cedar chest full of craft kits. "I'd pull out a crewel kit and do it while I stayed there," Chrissy says. She spent hours trying to decipher a cabled afghan her aunt had made. She'd drift off to sleep

Young Chrissy with her mom.

tracing its patterns and listening to the blue bug zapper on the neighbor's porch.

As a grown-up, Chrissy's own porch and domain have inherited a lot from Aitkin and Artis and Marsha. Her Portland house sits on a street leafy with cherry and hawthorn trees, and her backyard is the playground for kids, husband, cats, rabbits, and chickens. Inside, she blogs about a delicious red colorway by an indie dye company, likening it to the local strawberries she spent the day turning into jam, and dreams up patterns with names like Moonflower, Winter Branches, and Walk in the Woods, in an abundance that would make nature blush. She's designed and published hundreds of patterns by now, and her creativity is as central to her life as green is to a garden. ✄

A case in point, Chrissy's Twining Vines Pillow on page 89 reflects her sensitivity to the natural world.

DO YOUR THING,
LET IT TAKE OVER YOUR LIFE

Adrian Bizilia

BROWSE THROUGH ADRIAN BIZILIA'S DESIGNS ON-line at Twist Collective or on her website, Hello Yarn, and you may be transported deep into a magical wood or to sea on a pirate ship. She adorns her detailed mitten and hat designs with beetles, squirrels, fiddlehead ferns, and snails. A scarf appears lined with wood grain crafted with two colors of yarn. Mushrooms march across pulse warmers, calling to mind the colorful tea towels of the 1960s and 1970s. Skull and crossbones pattern a hat in an unexpected use of stranded color knitting. It's a kind of whimsy that takes a knitter into a realm of fantasy, or perhaps back to childhood and the warm glow of a beloved kitchen. At least, it does for Adrian.

Adrian fondly remembers her grandmother Marge's 1970s kitchen and, particularly, its eternally full candy drawer. The kitchen was situated inside a foursquare Colonial house on a quiet street in small-town Pennsylvania, and as Adrian speaks of it, it's easy to picture the warm light and comfort of this well-loved place. When she describes her grandmother, she paints a picture so vivid one can almost see her, tall and neat, wiping her hands on the apron tied around her waist, finished canning for the day and ready to turn her attention to other important matters—like handing out homemade popcorn balls to her grandchildren, or knitting.

At 12:30 every afternoon, Marge set aside her work to sit in front of the TV and knit—for four hours, without fail. Until 4:30, there was nothing else but knitting.

"It's okay to do it as much as you want" was the message that came through to Adrian, who made pom-poms at Marge's feet. "Do your thing. Let it take over your life."

And so Adrian did.

She emulated her grandma's work ethic, and, later in life, her knitting. She updated Marge's signature scratchy sweaters and mittens tied with string to create her own contemporary twists on colorwork and the mitten form.

But while her grandma may have taught Adrian about happy obsession—and the beauty of stranded color and the utility of mittens—she never did successfully teach her to knit. She tried several times over the years, when Adrian visited her house after school and when Adrian briefly lived with her as a girl, but it never stuck. "I always wanted to knit with her," pines Adrian. "I just sucked at it. So she gave me her pom-pom maker, and I sat and made pom-pom animals by her side."

Years later, in 2001, Adrian learned knitting from a book and, like her grandma, spent hours every day practicing her craft. She turned out a sweater a week in her early days.

Eventually, Adrian's obsession extended to making yarn. She is an influential dyer whose hand-dyed sock yarn was among the first of its kind in the early 2000s; Adrian was at the forefront of a major surge in indie yarns worldwide. Saturated with color, each skein is like a glimpse into a lovely space that Adrian has imagined: a sunlit glade, a snowy field, or the intimate corners of

Adrian's grandmother, Marge, who taught Adrian the value of making time for creative passions.

a home. She even gives knitters a peek into the bright secret of that ever-full candy drawer. Her colorways have evocative names like Needle and Cone, Embroidery, Dried Leaves, and Candied Peel.

Certainly, her grandmother's knitting ethic got her started. Adrian learned from Marge to immerse herself in her craft, obsess happily and without guilt, and not only make things, but make a *lot*. In fact, it now seems like all the rooms in Adrian's western Massachusetts farmhouse—where she works and lives with her husband, Mark, and dog, Pippa—as well as her hours and days, are devoted to creativity. She gardens, cooks, preserves, spins, dyes, knits, and blogs about it all at Hello Yarn. Her old house is a place she is always creating. It's always changing and full of fiber. One can almost picture Adrian in her kitchen there, wiping her hands on her own vintage apron, popcorn balls at the ready. ✄

At 12:30 every afternoon, Marge set aside her work to sit in front of the TV and knit—for four hours, without fail. Until 4:30, there was nothing else but knitting.

LESSON ONE: FEARLESS CREATIVITY

Kirsten Kapur

K IRSTEN KAPUR IS LIKE AN ARTIST WITH A BIG BOX of crayons. She spreads them out and discovers eye-opening combinations, with colors touching and enlivening one another in unexpected ways. But instead of Crayolas, her medium is yarn. In her knitting design work—seen on her blog, Through the Loops, and online via *Knitty*, KnitPicks, and Ravelry—Kirsten displays her mastery at manipulating tint, hue, line, and geometry.

Though Kirsten's presence as a designer is relatively new (her first online pattern was published in *Knitty* magazine in 2007), she has a lifetime of creative experience, having grown up in a large family where fearless invention was the norm.

Kirsten's mother was never without a knitting or sewing project, and as a young woman, she made her own stylish clothes. "In photos of her in her twenties, she looks like a fashion model with her willowy frame," Kirsten recounts. My father took many beautiful photos of her." A creative force himself, her dad had built his own darkroom at the age of twelve.

Kirsten figures that one of her female relatives—an aunt or grandmother—taught her to knit, but she doesn't remember specifics. "It was just something we all did in my family," she says. When she graduated from college with a fine arts degree, she landed a job in New York's garment industry. She worked there throughout the 1980s, researching trends, shopping for fabrics, inventing concepts, and drawing up specs for the oddly pieced, geometric clothes that were popular then. In 2007, wanting to invest more creative time at home, she took those apparel industry skills and began shifting her career to hand knitting design, diving into the online world of blogs and Ravelry. Just a few years later, it's her full-time job.

Today she engages knitters with her confident and unusual pairings—bold stripes and delicate lace together in one shawl, gloves knit sideways, and classic stitch patterns rendered in giant gauges (in one pattern, four super-sized leaves span the whole back of a six-foot-long stole). "You cannot be fearful," she says of creativity. "This was instilled in me from early childhood."

The main source of this lesson was a trio of great-aunts—strong figures in Kirsten's life, whom she speaks of with delight and affection. Born in the early twentieth century, two of the aunts went to the Rhode Island School of Design and were painters. All three knit, crocheted, sewed, smocked, and did needlepoint, embroidery, and cross-stitch. They grew sweeping perennial borders and made spectacular flower arrangements. Kirsten was especially impressed by the concrete patio at her aunts' Rhode Island home. One of them had adorned it with tiles and embossed it with the textures of bottle caps and coins, and little Kirsten, who visited every summer from her home in New Jersey, was fascinated by it. "If there was something they wanted to make or do, they didn't let not knowing the technique stop them," she says. "They simply learned what they needed to execute the idea. I think that was the biggest message that I got from them, to let the idea lead the way to the craft." ✄

Kirsten's grandmother Anna (top left) and her three awesome great aunts, Teresa, Mary, and Dorothy.

Kirsten's two cowl patterns on page 91 are a great way to start exploring your own fearless color sense.

FAMILY TRUNK PROJECT

Emily Johnson

MILY JOHNSON IS A SELF-TAUGHT KNITWEAR designer whose family stories come to life in the stitches of her designs. Reaching back to her great-grandparents' generation, she captures her ancestors' essence in knitted form—their loves, struggles, histories, trades, and homes. In 2008, she published the first of her family-inspired designs online in a collection she calls the Family Trunk Project.

Rather than updating garments her family members actually wore, Emily designs new ones based on their individual spirits, personalities, and stories. A slinky, bias-knit, Deco-inspired shell recalls her great-grandmother Maxine Elliott, whose bittersweet life included voyages to Hawaii and Shanghai. An intriguingly shaped tunic evokes Hawaiian culture in the 1930s and pays homage to the pineapple industry in which her great-grandfather, Charles Victor Morine, distinguished himself.

For each knitting design, Emily writes an accompanying essay that is brimming with tenderness, respect, and history. In collaboration with her partner, David Galli, a photographer and Web designer, the patterns and essays are published together on a Family Trunk Project website; some have also appeared online in *Knitty* and Twist Collective.

Emily's knitting has always been entwined with family, from the moment she sat beside her mother in a beginner's class in the mid-1990s. She was in middle school, during what she calls "that really narrow window of time before high-schoolers get embarrassed to hang out with their moms." Emily's mother was hooked on knitting from the start, but Emily stuck to designing and sewing her own clothes. "I was an oddball," she says. "I wanted to wear things that weren't readily available." But after graduating from college in 2004 with a degree in English literature, Emily tried knitting again, and this time she "flew off the handle" with it, diving immediately into inventing her own concepts, designs, and technical feats.

Emily approaches knitting design with the same confident skill and precision she first developed as an amateur seamstress, though she is not formally trained in design or garment making. She says her teenage sewing experience has made everything about knitting design seem less intimidating to her now, and she finds yarn to be far more forgiving than fabric. "There are fewer heartbreaking disasters," she says. "You can rip out, soak yarn. It makes me feel like I can just try everything."

Emily's grandmother, Betty Jean, and grandfather, Warren.

Emily began her Family Trunk Project in 2007, when she was twenty-six years old and starting to learn about her family members and ancestors with a new maturity. "Once I was recognized as an adult, the other adults opened up about family stories, some fascinating and compelling, some perhaps less savory than what I'd been told as a child." This new understanding began coalescing in her mind as a creative project in which she could tell family members' stories with knits.

Emily had always been interested in vintage clothing and fascinated with how clothes evoke times and characters so immediately and vividly.

In 2007, she started sketching out her family tree, then set out to research each family member and create sweaters, socks, and shawls—whatever was inspired by the stories she unearthed—for the fourteen people who made up her parents, grandparents, and great-grandparents.

For each project, Emily sifts through family photos and interviews family members, and she researches historic and census records as well as fashion from the relevant era. A design grows from this research, and from months of consideration about the family member's personality and spirit. She published the first of these works in 2008, and with nine out of fourteen designs now completed, Emily seems astounded that she's already more than halfway done.

Perhaps her favorite project so far represents her father's mother, Betty Jean McNeil, for whom she designed a tailored cardigan. "It was the most powerful emotional process for me," she says of creating the design and writing the accompanying essay. Emily recalls her grandmother as a "kind yet fiery companion who sat with me for hours in my favorite room—the tiny, nestlike one under the eaves—listening attentively as I described the fantastic worlds of my imagination." Betty died when Emily was in high school, at an age when young people are really self-involved, and she didn't take the time to grieve for Betty then. Working on her history and designing with her spirit in mind made memories come flooding back and made Emily feel close to her.

Today, Emily sells her knitting patterns for several dollars a pop—or for stories. At her Family Trunk Project website, knitters can buy a pattern in return for a prescribed number of pages of their own family history. She says about 10 percent of her pattern sales are bought this way, in lieu of money. The stories are of unexpectedly high quality, the system seeming to "self-select for people who enjoy writing." She's heard from a knitter whose grandparents are from the same tiny Irish village in which she still lives, and she received a transcript of an oral history from a knitter's grandmother on the Mexican border. "They are touching stories, reminiscences of people gone," she says.

Emily's work shows that stitches are as capable as words at telling a human tale, and that a deftly designed sweater can bring a loved one's personality to life. The Betty Jean McNeil cardigan certainly does. With its crisp tailoring and fitted, argyle-patterned bust, it speaks of a woman who was lively, straightforward, and a bit driven. Emily writes that Betty Jean told her once, "'The only things I regret are the ones I didn't do.' Then she looked at me and said, 'So do them.' Those words still play themselves out in my head whenever I'm feeling intimidated at the idea of trying something new." ✄

Emily's sock design on page 119 evokes the flowers of the Hawaiian islands where her great-grandparents lived.

Inspired Knits ✁

KEEPSAKE SCARF

BY RODGER P. MURRY

Perhaps the most basic and beloved knitting project of all is the humble striped scarf. This one invites you to dive into your stash and give new life to leftovers from projects gone by, or give a meaningful and pretty purpose to inherited yarn. Unlike most striped scarves, which are knit flat, this one is worked in the round so its stripes are thinner and more delicate than usual, and there is no "wrong" side to show.

FINISHED MEASUREMENTS
5" wide x 80" long

YARN
Cascade Yarns Cascade 220 (100% Peruvian highland wool; 220 yards / 100 grams): 3 hanks #8407 Oyster (MC)

Varying amounts (less than 1 hank) of the following:

Cascade Yarns Greenland (100% superwash merino; 137 yards / 100 grams): #3518 Blue Hawaii (A), #3520 Camel (B), and #3537 Sapphire (C)

Cascade Yarns Pastaza (50% llama / 50% wool; 132 yards / 100 grams): #084 Teal Heather (D) and #052 Forest (E)

Cascade Yarns Venezia Worsted (70% merino wool / 30% silk; 219 yards / 100 grams): #151 Black Forest (F), #163 Buttercup (G), and #101 White Heaven (H)

Cascade Yarns Sierra (80% pima cotton / 20% wool; 191 yards / 100 grams): #47 Bermuda Blue (I) and #407 Water Lily (J)

NEEDLES
One set of five double-pointed needles (dpn) size US 6 (4 mm)

Change needle size if necessary to obtain correct gauge.

GAUGE
26 sts and 35 rnds = 4" (10 cm) in Stockinette stitch (St st) (knit every rnd)

Note: Gauge is not essential for this project.

SCARF

Using MC, CO 66 sts. Join for working in the rnd, being careful not to twists sts; pm for beginning of rnd. Begin St st (knit every rnd); work even until piece measures 2" from the beginning.

Change to contrasting color of your choice; work even for 1 rnd. Alternating 1 rnd of MC with 1 rnd of contrasting color of your choice (see photo), work even until piece measures 78" from the beginning, or to 2" less than desired length. *Note: When changing colors, do not cut yarn if you will be working several alternating rows with the same colors; run colors not in use up inside of piece.*

Change to A; work even until piece measures 80" from the beginning. BO all sts. Block as desired.

VINTAGE GLOVES

BY ROBIN MELANSON

When Robin Melanson was around twelve years old, her grandma Margaret knit her a green acrylic vest in raspberry stitch. Although Margaret's knitting was not to Robin's taste, Margaret was a skilled knitter, and passed her talent along to her daughter and granddaughters. Today, Robin works with more understated grace than her grandma, often finding inspiration in the enchanting styles of the 1940s. Robin thinks her grandma might have worn delicate gloves like these as a young woman—before her passion for acrylic bobbles set in.

SIZES
Small (Medium, Large)

FINISHED MEASUREMENTS
Approximately 7 (7¾, 8¼)" circumference

YARN
St-Denis Nordique (100% wool; 150 yards / 50 grams): 2 balls #5812 Honey Glaze

NEEDLES
One set of five double-pointed needles (dpn) size US 3 (3.25 mm)
Change needle size if necessary to obtain correct gauge.

NOTIONS
Stitch markers; cable needle (cn); waste yarn

GAUGE
26 sts and 34 rows = 4" (10 cm) in Stockinette stitch (St st)

LEFT GLOVE

CUFF

CO 64 (64, 80) sts, divide evenly among 4 needles [16-16-16-16 (16-16-16-16, 20-20-20-20)]. Join for working in the rnd, being careful not to twist sts; pm for beginning of rnd.

Next Rnd: Begin Chart A; work Rnds 1-7 once—48 (48, 60) sts remain.

Next Rnd: Change to Chart B: work Rnds 1-10 once, then Rnds 11 and 12 six times—44 (44, 55) sts remain.

Next Rnd: Knit, decrease (increase, decrease) 0 (4, 3) sts evenly around—44 (48, 52) sts. Purl 1 rnd. Knit 5 rnds. Purl 1 rnd. Knit 1 rnd. Cuff should measure approximately 3½".

Shape Hand
Next Rnd: [K22 (24, 26), M1-l] twice—46 (50, 54) sts. Knit 2 rnds.

Shape Thumb
Increase Rnd 1: K21 (23, 25), pm, M1-l, k2, M1-r, pm, knit to end—48 (52, 56) sts. Knit 2 rnds.

Increase Rnd 2: Knit to first marker, sm, M1-l, knit to next marker, M1-r, sm, knit to end—50 (54, 58) sts.

Repeat Increase Rnd 2 every 3 rnds 5 (5, 6) times—60 (64, 70) sts. Knit 1 rnd.

Next Rnd: Knit to first marker, transfer next 16 (16, 18) sts to waste yarn for Thumb, removing markers CO 2 sts over gap, knit to end—46 (50, 54) sts remain. Work even in St st for 11 (12, 12) rnds, or until piece reaches base of pinkie finger, ending 5 (6, 6) sts before end of rnd.

Divide for Fingers

Pinkie Finger: Transfer next 10 (12, 12) sts [last 5 (6, 6) sts of rnd and first 5 (6, 6) sts of next rnd] to waste yarn for Pinkie Finger, removing marker, pm, CO 2 sts over gap, knit to 5 (6, 6) sts before marker.

Ring Finger: Transfer next 12 (14, 14) sts [5 (6, 6) sts from back of hand, 2 CO sts from Pinkie, and 5 (6, 6) sts from palm] to waste yarn, removing marker, pm, CO 2 sts over gap, knit to 6 (6, 7) sts before marker.

Middle Finger: Transfer next 14 (14, 16) sts [6 (6, 7) sts from back of hand, 2 CO sts from Ring Finger, and 6 (6, 7) sts from palm] to waste yarn, removing marker, pm, CO 2 sts over gap—16 (16, 18) sts remain for Index Finger.

INDEX FINGER

Work in St st for 26 (27, 28) rnds, or until piece is long enough to cover tip of index finger.

Decrease Rnd: *K2tog; repeat from * to end—8 (8, 9) sts remain. Cut yarn, leaving a 6" tail. Draw through remaining sts, pull tight and fasten off, with tail to the inside.

MIDDLE FINGER

Transfer sts from waste yarn to dpns. Rejoin yarn; pick up and knit 2 sts from sts CO between Index and Middle Fingers—16 (16, 18) sts. Join for working in the rnd; pm for beginning of rnd. Work in St st until piece is long enough to cover tip of middle finger. Complete as for Index Finger.

RING FINGER

Transfer sts from waste yarn to dpns. Rejoin yarn; pick up and knit 2 sts from sts CO between Middle and Ring Fingers—14 (16, 16) sts. Join for working in the rnd; pm for beginning of rnd. Work in St st until piece is long enough to cover tip of ring finger. Complete as for Index Finger.

PINKIE FINGER

Transfer sts from waste yarn to dpns. Rejoin yarn; pick up and knit 2 sts from sts CO between Ring and Pinkie Fingers—12 (14, 14) sts. Join for working in the rnd; pm for beginning of rnd. Work in St st until piece is long enough to cover tip of pinkie finger. Complete as for Index Finger.

THUMB

Transfer sts from waste yarn to dpns. Rejoin yarn; pick up and knit 2 sts from sts CO over gap—18 (18, 20) sts. Join for working in the rnd; pm for beginning of rnd. Work in St st for 22 (23, 24) rnds, or until piece is long enough to cover tip of thumb. Complete as for Index Finger.

RIGHT GLOVE

Work as for Left Glove to beginning of Thumb Shaping, beginning Charts A and B as indicated.

Shape Thumb

Increase Rnd 1: K23 (25, 27), pm, M1-l, k2, M1-r, pm, knit to end—48 (52, 56) sts. Knit 2 rnds.

Complete as for Left Glove, beginning with Increase Rnd 2, and working fingers in the same order, reversing terms for "palm" and "back of hand".

FINISHING

Use tails to close gaps between fingers. Block as desired.

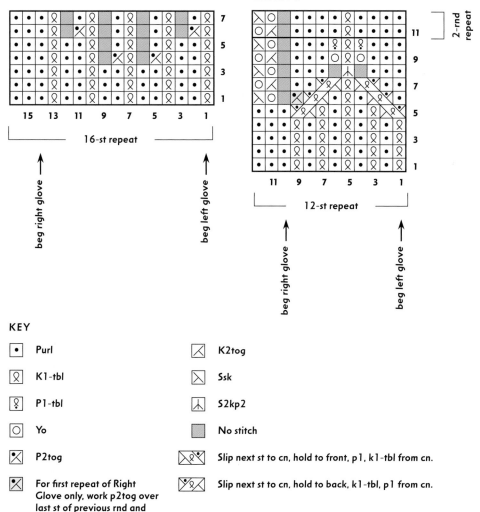

CHART A

7
5
3
1

15 13 11 9 7 5 3 1

16-st repeat

beg right glove →

beg left glove →

CHART B

2-rnd repeat

11
9
7
5
3
1

11 9 7 5 3 1

12-st repeat

beg right glove →

beg left glove →

KEY

• Purl	K2tog
K1-tbl	Ssk
P1-tbl	S2kp2
O Yo	No stitch
P2tog	Slip next st to cn, hold to front, p1, k1-tbl from cn.
For first repeat of Right Glove only, work p2tog over last st of previous rnd and first st of next rnd; reposition marker to before p2tog. Left Glove is worked as shown.	Slip next st to cn, hold to back, k1-tbl, p1 from cn.

CONCETTA CARDIGAN

BY CIRILIA ROSE

An update of a family heirloom, this shimmery cardigan is modeled after one that designer Cirilia Rose inherited from her great-grandmother, Concetta. Concetta knit hers in a pale pink wool-nylon blend that held up to the thousands of iridescent sequins she worked into every right side row. Cirilia—a member of the design team at Berroco—chose a lush and light alpaca yarn and went a little easier on the sparkle for this modern version.

SIZES
X-Small (Small, Medium, Large, X-Large)

FINISHED MEASUREMENTS
30 (34, 38, 42, 46)" bust

YARN
Berroco Ultra Alpaca Fine (50% wool / 30% nylon / 20% super fine alpaca; 433 yards / 100 grams): 3 (3, 4, 5, 5) hanks #1294 Turquoise Mix

NEEDLES
One 32" (80 cm) long circular (circ) needle size US 7 (4.5 mm)

One 16" (40 cm) long circular needle size US 6 (4 mm)

One set of five double-pointed needles (dpn) size US 6 (4 mm)

Change needle size if necessary to obtain correct gauge.

GAUGE
22 sts and 24 rows = 4" (10 cm) in Stockinette stitch (St st), using larger needle

NOTIONS
Stitch markers; yarn bobbins (optional); waste yarn; approximately 1320 (1420, 1560, 1700, 1800) sequins to match; sewing needle with eye large enough to fit yarn, but fine enough to fit through sequins; four ¾" buttons

STITCH PATTERNS
1x1 Rib (worked flat) (multiple of 2 sts + 1; 2-row repeat)

Row 1: Slip 1, *k1, p1; repeat from * to last 2 sts, k2.

Row 2: Slip 1, knit the knit sts and purl the purl sts as they face you.

Repeat Row 2 for 1x1 Rib (worked flat).

1x1 Rib (worked in-the-rnd) (multiple of 2 sts; 1-rnd repeat)

All Rnds: *K1, p1; repeat from * to end.

Seed Stitch (multiple of 2 sts; 1-row repeat)

Row 1 (WS): Slip 1, *k1, p1; repeat from * to end.

Row 2: Slip 1, knit the purl sts and purl the knit sts as they face you.

Repeat Row 2 for Seed Stitch.

The Body ribbing and bands and the Sleeve cuffs are worked with two strands of yarn held together. To make it easier to work the Body ribbing and Sleeve cuffs, wind a center pull ball of yarn so you can use a strand from the inside of the ball and a strand from the outside. To make it easier to work the Front bands, wind two bobbins of yarn, one for each Front. When working the bands, work with the strand from the bobbin and the strand from the yarn ball; when changing to work across the Body, drop the bobbin strand and continue with the yarn ball strand.

Prepare Yarn with Sequins: Thread yarn through sewing needle, then string 10 sequins onto yarn, making sure that if you are using cupped sequins, all the cups face the same direction. After the initial 10 sequins are strung, there is no need to count the remaining sequins one by one. Measure the width of the 10 sequins you have strung; divide the number of sequins needed by 10, then multiply that amount by the width of the 10 strung sequins to get the approximate width of strung sequins you will need. You might wish to add 20 or more sequins to the amount suggested, to make sure you don't run out.

BODY

Using larger needles and 2 strands of yarn held together, CO 209 (231, 253, 275, 297) sts. Begin 1x1 Rib (worked flat); work even for 1", ending with a RS row. Knit 1 row. Drop 1 strand of yarn and cut it.

(RS) Join yarn from bobbin and, with 2 strands of yarn held together, work 7 sts as established, drop bobbin strand, work in St st (beginning with a knit row) to last 7 sts, join yarn from second bobbin, work as established to end. Work even until piece measures 1½" from the beginning, ending with a WS row. Place markers 47 (53, 58, 64, 69) sts in from each side.

Shape Body
Decrease Row (RS): Decrease 4 sts this row, then every 6 (8, 8, 10, 10) rows 7 times, as follows: [Work to 4 sts before marker, ssk, k4, k2tog] twice, work to end—177 (199, 221,

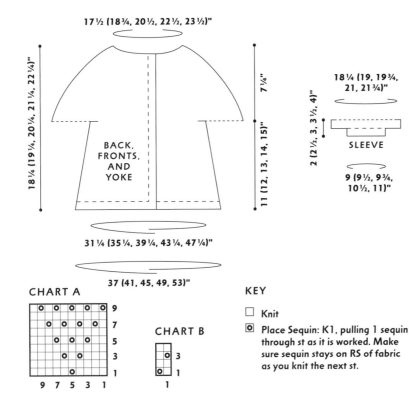

17½ (18¾, 20½, 22½, 23½)"

18¼ (19¼, 20¼, 21¼, 22¼)"

7¼"

11 (12, 13, 14, 15)"

BACK, FRONTS, AND YOKE

31¼ (35¼, 39¼, 43¼, 47¼)"

37 (41, 45, 49, 53)"

18¼ (19, 19¾, 21, 21¾)"

2 (2½, 3, 3½, 4)"

SLEEVE

9 (9½, 9¾, 10½, 11)"

CHART A

9
7
5
3
1

9 7 5 3 1

CHART B

3
1

1

KEY

☐ Knit

◉ Place Sequin: K1, pulling 1 sequin through st as it is worked. Make sure sequin stays on RS of fabric as you knit the next st.

243, 265) sts remain. Work even until piece measures 11 (12, 13, 14, 15)", or to desired length from the beginning, ending with a RS row.

Shape Armholes

(WS) [Work to 5 sts before marker, BO 10 sts, removing marker] twice, work to end. Place sts on holder and set aside.

SLEEVES

Using dpns and 2 strands of yarn held together, CO 50 (52, 54, 58, 60) sts. Join for working in the rnd, being careful not to twist sts; pm for beginning of rnd. Begin 1x1 Rib (worked in-the-rnd); work even for 4 rnds. Purl 1 rnd.

Next Rnd: Change to single strand of yarn. *K1, yo; repeat from * to end—100 (104, 108, 116, 120) sts. Change to smaller circ needle and St st (knit every rnd); work even until piece measures 2 (2 ½, 3, 3 ½, 4)" from the beginning.

Next Rnd: Knit to last 5 sts, BO next 10 sts, removing marker—90 (94, 98, 106, 110) sts remain. Transfer sts from first Sleeve to waste yarn; set aside. Leave sts from second Sleeve on needle for Yoke.

YOKE

With RS facing, work across Right Front sts, Right Sleeve sts, Back

sts, Left Sleeve sts, then work to end—337 (367, 397, 435, 465) sts. Working in St st, work even for 7 rows.

Shape Yoke

(RS) Work 7 sts, *k3, k2tog; repeat from * to last 10 (10, 10, 8, 8) sts, work to end—273 (297, 321, 351, 375) sts remain. Work even for 1 row, increase 1 (0, 3, 3, 0) sts or decrease 0 (3, 0, 0, 1) st(s) evenly spaced across row, working increases or decreases outside of Front bands—274 (294, 324, 354, 374) sts. Cut yarn from ball; do not cut yarn from bobbins.

(RS) Join yarn strung with sequins; you will work this yarn together with bobbin yarn for bands, but do not work sequins on bands. Work 7 sts as established, work Chart A to last 7 sts, work to end. Continue in pattern as established for 7 rows.

Buttonhole Row (RS): Slip 1, k1, p1, k1, yo, k2tog, p1, work to end.

Decrease Row 1 (WS): Work 10 (10, 8, 10, 10) sts, *p2tog, p2; repeat from * to last 8 sts, work to end—210 (225, 247, 270, 285) sts remain.

(RS) Change to Chart B; work even for 11 rows, working Buttonhole Row on a RS row 8 rows above first buttonhole.

Decrease Row 2 (WS): Continuing to work Chart B, work 8 (8, 9, 8, 8) sts, *p2tog, p1; repeat from * to last 7 sts, work to end—145 (155, 170, 185, 195) sts remain. Continuing to work Chart B, work even for 7 rows, working Buttonhole Row on a RS row 8 rows above second buttonhole.

Decrease Row 3 (WS): Continuing to work Chart B, work 8 (9, 9, 9, 7) sts, *p2tog, p1; repeat from * to last 8 sts, work to end—102 (109, 119, 129, 135) sts remain.

Note: You will not be working with sequins for the remainder of the Yoke; slide any remaining sequins out of the way as you work.

(RS) Continuing with 2 strands held together, p7, drop bobbin yarn and cut it, purl with single strand of yarn to last 7 sts, with 2 strands of yarn, purl to end.

(WS) Continuing with 2 strands of yarn held together across entire row, begin Seed st; work even for 2 rows.

Buttonhole Row (WS): Work to last 6 sts, k2tog, yo, work to end. Work even for 3 rows. BO all sts in pattern.

FINISHING

Sew underarm seams. Block gently, being careful of sequins. Sew buttons opposite buttonholes.

FAMILY TREE AFGHAN

BY LARISSA BROWN

Just like my grandmother Olive, I love to make afghans. Nanny favored Red Heart yarns in rusts, avocados, and pinks, while I tend to prefer natural fibers and a broader palette. For this one, I chose fingering-weight wool in the colors of autumn in my New Jersey hometown. This is a a perfect project for using up inherited or special scraps and oddballs, or for indulging in all-new yarn. Made of leaf-shaped segments that are sewn together, it's certain to earn heirloom status quickly.

FINISHED MEASUREMENTS

Leaves: 6 ¾" wide x 7" high, after heavy blocking

Afghan: Approximately 41" each side; approximately 48" wide x 66" long, measured from point to point

YARN

Pico Accuardi Dyeworks Marco Bambino (100% superwash merino wool; 380 yards / 100 grams): 4 hanks each Brandon's Rainy Day, Aunt Honey, Fair Soren Claire, Stumptown Brown, Gwen's Goldrush, and Bleeding Heart. *Note: Each 100-gram hank yields approximately 5 Leaves.*

NEEDLES

One pair straight needles size US 7 (4.5 mm)

Change needle size if necessary to obtain correct gauge.

NOTIONS

Stitch marker; 7" square of cardboard or plastic

GAUGE

20 sts and 32 rows = 4" (10 cm) in Stockinette stitch (St st), using 2 strands of yarn held together, before blocking

18 sts and 32 rows = 4" (10 cm) in Stockinette stitch, using 2 strands of yarn held together, after heavy blocking

Note: The Leaves are stretched horizontally during blocking, but the height does not change.

LEAVES (make 110 in colors of your choice)

Using 2 strands held together, CO 2 sts.

Row 1 (WS): Purl.

Row 2: Slip 1 knitwise, M1-r, k1— 3 sts.

Row 3: Slip 1 purlwise, p1-tbl, p1.

Row 4: Slip 1 knitwise, M1-r, pm, k1, M1-l, k1—5 sts.

Row 5: Slip 1 purlwise, p1-tbl, purl to last 2 sts, p1-tbl, p1.

Row 6: Slip 1 knitwise, k1-tbl, knit to marker, M1-r, sm, k1, M1-l, knit to last 2 sts, k1-tbl, k1—7 sts.

Rows 7-32: Repeat Rows 5 and 6—33 sts after Row 32.

Row 33: Repeat Row 5.

Row 34: Slip 1 knitwise, ssk, knit to last 3 sts, k2tog, k1—31 sts remain.

Rows 35-60: Repeat Rows 33 and 34—5 sts remain.

Row 61: Repeat Row 5.

Row 62: Slip 1 knitwise, s2kp2, k1—3 sts remain.

Row 63: Slip 1 purlwise, p2.

Row 64: S2kp2—1 st remains. Fasten off.

FINISHING

Block all Leaves to 6 ¾" at widest point x 7" high. *Note: You may wish to use a template cut from cardboard or plastic, to make blocking quicker and more uniform.*

Assembly: When Leaves are blocked and dry, arrange them in a diamond shape, with the base of each Leaf resting against the top edges of two others (see photo). Sew Leaves together. Reblock completed Afghan if desired.

ICE SKATING CAPE

BY COSETTE CORNELIUS-BATES

This snowy, swingy cape is an update of a 1960s handknit heirloom that made its way into the hands of designer Cosette Cornelius-Bates. It came with a story. The original was finished at the last minute so the knitter's daughter could wear it to an ice skating party. This contemporary remake is perfect for gifting and can be worn equally beautifully as a cape or skirt (see page 5).

SIZES
Small (Medium, Large)

FINISHED MEASUREMENTS
55¾ (72¼, 87½)" wide at widest point by 17" long

YARN
Cascade Yarns Ecological Wool (100% natural Peruvian wool; 478 yards / 250 grams): 2 (2, 3) hanks #8016 (MC)

NEEDLES
One 29" (70 cm) long or longer circular (circ) needle size US 10 (6 mm)

Change needle size if necessary to obtain correct gauge.

NOTIONS
Four 1" buttons; 1½ (1¾, 2) yards 1½" wide satin ribbon

GAUGE
18 sts and 22 rows = 4" (10 cm) in Stockinette stitch (St st)

STITCH PATTERN
Cape Pattern (any number of sts; 2-row repeat)

Row 1 (WS): K6, purl to last 6 sts, knit to end.

Row 2: Knit.

Repeat Rows 1 and 2 for Cape Pattern.

CAPE
Note: Piece is worked from the top down.

Using MC, CO 71 (89, 107) sts. Knit 3 rows.

Buttonhole Row (WS): K2, BO 2 sts, k1, purl to last 6 sts, k6. Work pattern as follows and, AT THE SAME TIME, repeat Buttonhole Row every 20 rows 3 times, casting on 2 sts over bound-off sts on the following row.

Eyelet Row (RS): K6, yo, k2tog, *k4 (5, 6), yo, k2tog; repeat from * to last 9 (11, 11) sts, k3 (4, 5), yo, knit to end, CO 2 sts over BO sts—72 (90, 108) sts.

(WS) Begin Cape Pattern; work even for 2 rows. Knit 1 row.

Shape Cape
Increase Row 1 (RS): K6, *k2, k1-f/b; repeat from * to last 6 sts, knit to end—92 (116, 140) sts. Work even in Cape Pattern for 6 rows. Knit 1 row. Work even in Cape Pattern for 4 rows.

Increase Row 2 (RS): K6, *k3, k1-f/b; repeat from * to last 6 sts, knit to end—112 (142, 172) sts. Work even in Cape Pattern for 8 rows. Knit 1 row.

Increase Row 3 (RS): K6, *k4, k1-f/b; repeat from * to last 6 sts, knit to end—132 (168, 204) sts. Work even in Cape Pattern for 5 rows.

Increase Row 4 (RS): K6, *k11, k1-f/b; repeat from * to last 18 sts, knit to end—141 (180, 219) sts. Work even in Cape Pattern for 8 rows. Knit 1 row. Work even in Cape Pattern for 23 rows. Knit 1 row.

Increase Row 5 (RS): K3 (0, 2), *k5, k1-f/b; repeat from * to last 6 (6, 7) sts, knit to end—163 (209, 254) sts.

(WS) Change to St st across all sts, beginning with a purl row; work even for 3 rows.

Increase Row 6 (RS): K3 (0, 2), *k6, M1-r, k1, M1-l; repeat from * to last 6 (6, 7) sts, knit to end—207 (267, 324) sts. Work in St st for 3 rows.

Increase Row 7 (RS): K3 (0, 2), *k6, M1-r, k3, M1-l; repeat from * to last 6 (6, 7) sts, knit to end—251 (325, 394) sts. Work in St st, beginning with a purl row, until piece measures 17" or to desired length from the beginning, ending with a RS row. Knit 1 row. BO all sts.

Block piece. Sew buttons opposite buttonholes.

Thread ribbon through eyelets in Eyelet Row. Embellish with pom poms or tassels (optional; see Special Techniques, page 000).

GRANDMA'S FAN DISHCLOTH

BY JUDY BECKER

Designer Judy Becker found inspiration for this washcloth in the antique lace medallions she inherited from her grandma and great-aunts, many of which featured flowers and fans. While those were made with a variety of methods—crochet, tatting, bobbin lace—this swirling cousin, which borrows from those motifs, is all knit. It's always amazing how something as simple as a dishcloth can warm up a kitchen when handmade.

FINISHED MEASUREMENTS
Approximately 9" diameter

YARN
Tahki Cotton Classic (100% mercerized cotton; 108 yards / 50 grams) 1 hank #3559 Butterscotch. *Note: One hank will make one Dishcloth, with yarn left over.*

NEEDLES
One set of five double-pointed needles (dpn) size US 3 (3.25 mm)

NOTIONS
Stitch marker

GAUGE
Not essential for this project.

DISHCLOTH

Using Judy's Magic CO (see Special Techniques, page 000) and a 12" tail, CO 2 sts onto each of two needles—4 sts.

Set-Up Rnd 1: Holding the tail and working yarn together, k4, keeping the sts on separate needles—8 loops.

Set-Up Rnd 2: Holding the tail and working yarn together, knit each individual loop, still keeping the sts on separate needles—16 loops. Drop tail.

Set-Up Rnd 3: Knit each individual loop, knitting 4 sts onto each of 4 needles—16 sts. Join for working in the rnd. Place marker for beginning of rnd. *Note: Since the tail is at the beginning of the rnd, you may omit placing a marker and simply use the location of the tail to indicate the beginning of the rnd.*

Rnd 1: *Yo, k2; repeat from * to end—24 sts.

Rnd 2: *K1-tbl, k2; repeat from * to end.

Rnd 3: *Yo, k3; repeat from * to end—32 sts.

Rnd 4: *K1-tbl, k3; repeat from * to end.

Rnd 5: *Yo, k4; repeat from * to end—40 sts.

Rnd 6: *K1-tbl, k4; repeat from * to end.

Rnd 7: *Yo, k5; repeat from * to end—48 sts.

Rnd 8: *K1-tbl, k5; repeat from * to end.

Rnd 9: *Yo, k6; repeat from * to end—56 sts.

Rnd 10: *K1-tbl, k6; repeat from * to end.

Rnd 11: *Yo, k7; repeat from * to end—64 sts.

Rnd 12: *K1-tbl, k7; repeat from * to end.

Rnd 13: *Yo, k8; repeat from * to end—72 sts.

Rnd 14: *K1-tbl, k8; repeat from * to end.

Rnd 15: *Yo, k9; repeat from * to end—80 sts.

Rnd 16: *K1-tbl, k9; repeat from * to end.

Rnd 17: *Yo, k10; repeat from * to end—88 sts.

Rnd 18: *K1-tbl, k10; repeat from * to end.

Rnd 19: *Yo, k11; repeat from * to end—96 sts.

Rnd 20: *K1-tbl, k11; repeat from * to end.

Note: You may work Rnds 21-39 from the following text or from the Chart. Knit all yarnovers in the following rnds through the front loop to keep them open.

Rnd 21: *Yo, k9, k2tog, yo, k1; repeat from * to end—104 sts.

Rnds 22, 24, 26, and 28: Knit.

Rnd 23: *K1, yo, k8, k2tog, yo, k2; repeat from * to end—112 sts.

Rnd 25: *Yo, ssk, yo, k7, [k2tog, yo] twice, k1; repeat from * to end—120 sts.

Rnd 27: *K1, yo, ssk, yo, k6, [k2tog, yo] twice, k2; repeat from * to end—128 sts.

Rnd 29: *[Yo, ssk] twice, yo, k5, [k2tog, yo] 3 times, k1; repeat from * to end—136 sts.

Rnd 30: *K5, yo, k4, k2tog, yo, k6; repeat from * to end—144 sts.

Rnd 31: *K1, [yo, ssk] twice, k1, yo, k3, k2tog, yo, k1, [k2tog, yo] twice, k2; repeat from * to end—152 sts.

Rnd 32: *K7, yo, k2, k2tog, yo, k8; repeat from * to end—160 sts.

Rnd 33: *[Yo, ssk] 3 times, k2, yo, k1, k2tog, yo, k2, [k2tog, yo] 3 times, k1; repeat from * to end—168 sts.

Rnd 34: *K5, yo, ssk, k2, yo, k2tog, yo, k2, k2tog, yo, k6; repeat from * to end—176 sts.

Rnd 35: *K1, [yo, ssk] twice, k1, yo, ssk, k5, k2tog, yo, k1, [k2tog, yo] twice, k2; repeat from * to end.

Rnd 36: *K7, yo, k5, k2tog, yo, k8; repeat from * to end—184 sts.

Rnd 37: *[Yo, ssk] twice, yo, k12, [k2tog, yo] 3 times, k1; repeat from * to end—192 sts.

Rnd 38: *K5, yo, k11, k2tog, yo, k6; repeat from * to end—200 sts.

Rnd 39: *K1, yo, ssk, yo, k16, [k2tog, yo] twice, k2; repeat from * to end—208 sts.

Rnd 40: Knit.

Rnd 41: K11, [k3tog, k10, yo, sk2p, yo, k10] 7 times, k3tog, k10, yo, sk2p (removing marker), yo—192 sts remain.

Rnd 42: Knit. BO all sts loosely.

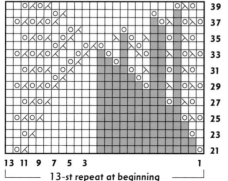

KEY

☐ Knit
◎ Yo
⊠ K2tog
⊠ Ssk
▨ No stitch

13-st repeat at beginning

ANGELINA SHRUG

BY JOAN McGOWAN-MICHAEL

This elegant shrug is designed to wrap you in an unbearably soft hug. Infused with Joan's mother's 1940s style, and modeled after the bed jackets of that era, it's equally lovely worn with a dress or with rough jeans and cowboy boots. The construction is deceptively simple. The body is worked in one piece and then folded in half and stitched up the sides, leaving space for the arms; the lace border is applied last.

SIZES
To fit bust sizes 34-36 (38-40, 42-44, 46-48)"

FINISHED MEASUREMENTS
17 ¾ (20, 22 ¼, 24 ¼)" wide x 12 (14, 15, 17)" long, sewn, before Lace Edging

YARN
Cascade Yarns Venezia Worsted (70% merino wool / 30% silk; 219 yards / 100 grams): 3 (4, 4, 5) hanks #132 Mouse (A)

Cascade Yarns Kid Seta (70% kid mohair / 30% silk; 230 yards / 25 grams): 3 (4, 4, 5) balls #405 Sand (B)

NEEDLES
One pair straight needles size US 7 (4.5 mm)

Change needle size if necessary to obtain correct gauge.

GAUGE
22 sts and 26 rows = 4" (10 cm) in Faggotting Stitch

NOTE
If bust size is larger than a B cup, add length to the ribbed portions at the beginning and end of the Body to obtain more coverage. Add approximately 1½" for each cup size above a B cup.

STITCH PATTERNS
2x2 Rib (multiple of 4 sts; 1-row repeat)

All Rows: *K2, p2; repeat from * to end.

Faggotting Stitch (multiple of 6 sts + 2; 2-row repeat—see Chart)

Row 1 (RS): *P2, k2, yo, k2tog; repeat from * to last 2 sts, p2.

Row 2: K2, *p2, yo, k2tog, k2; repeat from * to end.

Repeat Rows 1 and 2 for Faggotting Stitch.

French Lace Edging (multiple varies; 8-row repeat—see Chart)

Row 1 (RS): K3, yo, k2tog, k2, yo, k2tog, k4.

Row 2: K2, [yo] 3 times, [k2, yo, k2tog] twice, k2, slip 1, pick up and knit 1 st from edge of Body, psso—16 sts.

Row 3: K5, yo, k2tog, k2, yo, k2tog, [k1, p1, k1, p1] in triple yo, dropping 2 yos, k2—17 sts.

Row 4: K8, [yo, k2tog, k2] twice, slip 1, pick up and knit 1 st from edge of Body, psso.

Row 5: K5, yo, k2tog, k2, yo, k2tog, k6.

Row 6: K10, yo, k2tog, k2, yo, k2tog, slip 1, pick up and knit 1 st from edge of Body, psso.

Row 7: K3, yo, k2tog, k2, yo, k2tog, k8.

Row 8: BO 4 sts, knit to last st, slip 1, pick up and knit 1 st from edge of Body, psso—13 sts remain.

Repeat Rows 1–8 for French Lace Edging.

BODY

Using 1 strand each of A and B held together, CO 196 (220, 244, 268) sts. Begin 2x2 Rib; work even for 2 (3, 3, 4)" (or to desired length if your bust size is larger than a B cup—see Note), ending with a RS row.

(WS) *K2tog, p2tog; repeat from * to end—98 (110, 122, 134) sts remain.

(RS) Change to Faggoting st; work even until piece measures 20 (22, 24, 26)" from end of ribbing, ending with a WS row.

(RS) *K1-f/b; repeat from * to end—196 (220, 244, 268) sts.

(WS) Change to 2x2 Rib; work even until ribbing measures 2 (3, 3, 4)" (or to desired length if bust size is larger than a B cup). BO all sts in pattern.

Fold Body in half with CO and BO edges together; sew side edges together, beginning at CO/BO edges, and continuing approximately 4 (5, 5, 6)" up side edges.

EDGING

Using 1 strand each of A and B held together, CO 13 sts. Begin French Lace Edging (you may work pattern from text or Chart); work even for 1 row. With WS of Body facing, beginning at side seam, continue to work French Lace Edging along CO, then BO edge of Body, picking up and working 1 st from CO or BO edge together with the last st of every WS row of French Lace Edging, as indicated in pattern.

FINISHING

Block lightly, blocking Lace Edging well.

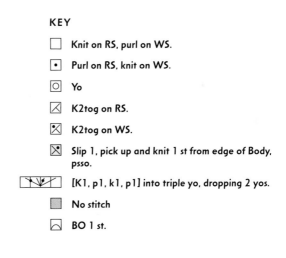

FAGGOTING STITCH

8-st repeat

2-row repeat

FRENCH LACE EDGING

8-row repeat

variable repeat

KEY

☐ Knit on RS, purl on WS.

• Purl on RS, knit on WS.

Ⓞ Yo

◺ K2tog on RS.

◸ K2tog on WS.

◺ Slip 1, pick up and knit 1 st from edge of Body, psso.

[K1, p1, k1, p1] into triple yo, dropping 2 yos.

▨ No stitch

⌒ BO 1 st.

TWINING VINES PILLOW

BY CHRISSY GARDINER

Every porch swing—or Adirondack chair or hammock—needs a pillow or two for kicking back with the crossword puzzle on Sunday afternoon or stargazing on a hot summer night. This one traces twining lines in a classic cable motif, which contrasts playfully with 1950s-style bark cloth backing. You can almost hear the crickets and taste the iced tea.

FINISHED MEASUREMENTS
approximately 18" square

YARN
Cascade Yarns Greenland (100% superwash merino; 137 yards / 100 grams): 3 hanks #3533 Tan

NEEDLES
One pair straight needles size US 7 (4.5 mm)

Change needle size if necessary to obtain correct gauge.

NOTIONS
Crochet hook size US G/6 (4 mm); cable needle (cn); 2 pieces of fabric 12 ½" x 18"; sewing machine (optional); sewing needle and thread; 18" square pillow form

GAUGE
26 sts and 30 rows = 4" (10 cm) over Cable Pattern from Chart

PILLOW FRONT
CO 118 sts. Begin Cable Pattern from Chart; work Rows 1 and 2 once, Rows 3-30 four times, then Rows 3-20 once. BO all sts in pattern. Do not fasten off final st; place st on crochet hook.

Crochet Edging
With RS facing, using crochet hook, ch 1, work 3 sc in upper left-hand corner of Pillow Front, then, working down left-hand edge of Front first, work sc around entire Front, working 3 sc for every 4 rows/sts, and turning corners by working 3 sc in each corner st. Join with slip st to first sc. Fasten off.

FINISHING
Block Front to measurements.

Fabric Back
Iron fabric and, if desired, sew around all edges of both pieces with a zig-zag st to prevent fraying. Fold one long edge of each piece ½" to WS and press. Sew each piece ¼" in from folded edge. Lay Front RS up on flat surface, then lay fabric pieces RS down on Front, with sewn edges overlapping in the middle. Pin all outside edges together. Using ³⁄₈" seam allowance, sew all edges of Pillow, backstitching in the corners for strength. Turn Pillow RS out and press seams. Insert pillow form.

CABLE PATTERN

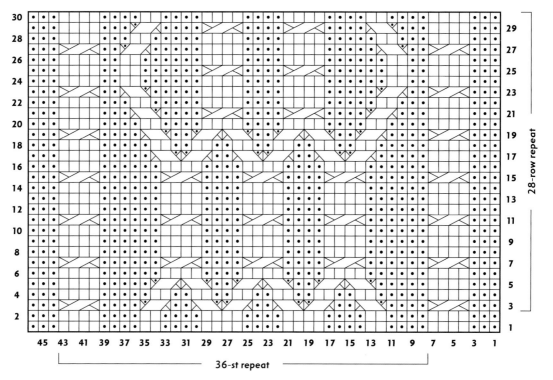

30 29
28 27
26 25
24 23
22 21
20 19
18 17
16 15
14 13
12 11
10 9
8 7
6 5
4 3
2 1

45 43 41 39 37 35 33 31 29 27 25 23 21 19 17 15 13 11 9 7 5 3 1

28-row repeat

36-st repeat

KEY

☐ Knit on RS, purl on WS.

• Purl on RS, knit on WS.

▷◁ Slip 2 sts to cn, hold to back, k2, k2 from cn.

◁ Slip 2 sts to cn, hold to front, p1, k2 from cn.

▷ Slip next st to cn, hold to back, k2, p1 from cn.

CRAYON COWLS

BY KIRSTEN KAPUR

Kirsten's great-aunts—Teresa, Mary, and Dorothy—were bold and fearless crafters, and they passed that spirit along to Kirsten. Kirsten's cowls are like a playground for creativity. Easy to knit, they are great projects for taking chances and experimenting with striking color combinations.

FINISHED MEASUREMENTS

26" circumference x 9" long

YARN

Cascade Yarns Venezia Worsted (70% merino wool / 30% silk; 219 yards / 100 grams): 1 hank each: Version 1: #151 Black Forest (A) and #174 Mulberry (B); Version 2: #174 Mulberry (A) and #104 Hot Pepper (B)

NEEDLES

One pair straight needles size US 7 (4.5 mm)

Change needle size if necessary to obtain correct gauge.

NOTIONS

Stitch markers; seven ¾" buttons

GAUGE

20 sts and 31 rows = 4" (10 cm) in pattern from Body for each Version

NOTES

In the instructions, you are told to slip the first stitch of every row. This will give the cowl a clean edge. To do this, insert the tip of the right-hand needle into the first stitch on the left-hand needle as if you were going to purl it. Now slip it onto the right-hand needle without doing anything to it. For the next stitch, bring the working yarn from the front to the back of the work, between the stitch on the left-hand needle and the stitch on the right-hand needle. You are now ready to knit the next stitch. Be careful not to pull the yarn too tight when knitting the second stitch, or the edge will not lie flat.

This pattern alternates two rows of each color throughout the pattern. There is no need to cut the yarn at the color changes. Simply carry the yarn up the side of the work. To do this, drop the yarn you are working with and pick up the next color. Since you are slipping the first stitch, bring the new color up to the inside of the old color. If you carry the yarn up in the same way on every color change, you will have a tidy edge. Be careful not to pull the yarn too tight when knitting the second stitch, or the edge will not lie flat.

COWL

Using A, CO 45 sts.

BUTTON BAND (both versions)

Rows 1 (RS) and 2: With A, slip 1, knit to end.

Rows 3 and 4: With B, slip 1, knit to end.

Rows 5-8: Repeat Rows 1-4, placing marker 4 sts in from each edge on last row.

BODY

Version 1

Row 1: With A, slip 1, knit to end, slipping markers.

Row 2: Slip 1, knit to first marker, sm, purl to next marker, sm, k4.

Rows 3 and 4: With B, slip 1, knit to end, slipping markers.

Work Rows 1-4 forty-five more times, then work Rows 1 and 2 once more, removing markers on last row.

Version 2

Row 1: With A, slip 1, knit to end, slipping markers.

Row 2: Slip 1, knit to first marker, sm, purl to next marker, sm, k4.

Rows 3 and 4: With B, slip 1, knit to end, slipping markers.

Rows 5 and 6: With A, slip 1, knit to first marker, sm, k1, *yo, k2tog; repeat from * to next marker, sm, k4.

Rows 7 and 8: Repeat Rows 3 and 4.

Work Rows 1-8 twenty-two more times, then work Rows 1 and 2 once more, removing markers on last row.

BUTTONHOLE BAND
(both versions)

Rows 1 and 2: With B, slip 1, knit to end.

Rows 3 and 4: With A, slip 1, knit to end.

Row 5 (Buttonhole Row): With B, slip 1, k3, [yo, k2tog, k4] 6 times, yo, k2tog, k3.

Row 6: Slip 1, knit to end.

Rows 7: With A, slip 1, knit to end. BO all sts.

FINISHING

Block as desired. Sew buttons opposite buttonholes.

FIDDLER'S MITTS

BY YSOLDA TEAGUE

Ysolda Teague's sweet mitts mix classic wool with a contemporary fingerless design and delicate picot edging. Pretty but sturdy, they invite the knitter to play with color combinations that might conjure up a walk in the woods at twilight or a picnic on a brilliant spring day. Ysolda named them for her grandfather, William, a Renaissance man who not only knit sweaters for young Ysolda but also made violins.

SIZES
Small (Large)

FINISHED MEASUREMENTS
6 ¼ (7 ¼)" circumference

YARN
Jamieson and Smith Shetland 2-ply Jumper Weight (100% Shetland wool; 130 yards / 25 grams): 1 skein each #82 Loch Maree (MC) and #FC50 Dusty Rose (A)

NEEDLES
Size Small: One set of four double-pointed needles (dpn) size US 2 (2.75 mm)

Size Large: One set of four double-pointed needles size US 2 ½ (3 mm)

Change needle size if necessary to obtain correct gauge.

NOTIONS
Stitch marker; waste yarn

GAUGE
Size Small: 32 sts and 36 rnds = 4" (10 cm) in Fair Isle Pattern from Mitt Chart, using smaller needles

Size Large: 28 sts and 32 rnds = 4" (10 cm) in Fair Isle Pattern from Mitt Chart, using larger needles

STITCH PATTERNS
1x1 Rib (multiple of 2 sts; 1-rnd repeat)

All Rnds: *K1, p1; repeat from * to end.

NOTE
Both sizes are worked exactly the same. The size Small is worked using the smaller needles; the size Large is worked using the larger needles.

RIGHT MITT
HAND

Using A and smaller (larger) needles required, CO 25 sts as follows: CO 5 sts using Cable CO (see Special Techniques, page 000), [BO 2 sts, slip st on right-hand needle back to left-hand needle, CO 4 sts using Cable CO] 11 times, BO 2 sts, slip st back to left-hand needle.

Row 1 (RS): K1-f/b; repeat from *
to end—50 sts. Divide sts among 3
needles [11-27-12]. Join for working
in the rnd, being careful not to twist
sts; pm for beginning of rnd.

Next Rnd: Change to MC; knit 1
rnd. Change to 1x1 Rib; work even
for 5 rnds.

Next Rnd: Begin Fair Isle Pattern
from Right Mitt Chart; work even
until Rnd 28 is complete.

Rnd 29: Work to Thumb sts, slip
next 9 sts onto waste yarn for
Thumb, using Backward Loop CO
(see Special Techniques, page 000),
[CO 1 st with MC, CO 1 st with A]
4 times, CO 1 st with MC, work to
end. Work even until entire Chart is
complete.

Next Rnd: Change to MC; knit 2
rnds. Change to 1x1 Rib; work even
for 6 rnds. BO all sts in pattern.

THUMB

Carefully remove waste yarn from
Thumb sts and place sts on dpn. Join
MC, pick up and knit 1 st between
sts on needle and CO sts, pick up and
knit 1 st in MC from first CO st, [pick
up and knit 1 st in A, pick up and knit
1 st in MC] 4 times across remaining
CO sts, pick up and knit 1 st in MC
between CO sts and sts on dpn—20
sts. Divide sts among 3 needles [6-7-
7]. Join for working in the rnd; pm for
beginning of rnd.

RIGHT MITT

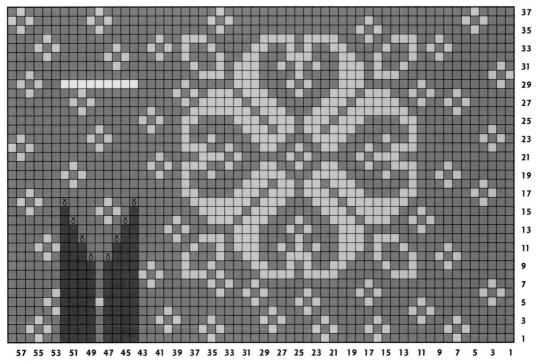

57 55 53 51 49 47 45 43 41 39 37 35 33 31 29 27 25 23 21 19 17 15 13 11 9 7 5 3 1

Next Rnd: Begin Thumb Chart; work even until entire Chart is complete.

Next Rnd: Change to MC; knit 2 rnds. Change to 1x1 Rib; work even for 2 rnds. BO all sts in pattern.

Work as for Right Mitt, dividing sts among 3 needles on Row 1 as follows: [12-27-11]; work Fair Isle Pattern from Left Mitt Chart.

FINISHING

Block as desired.

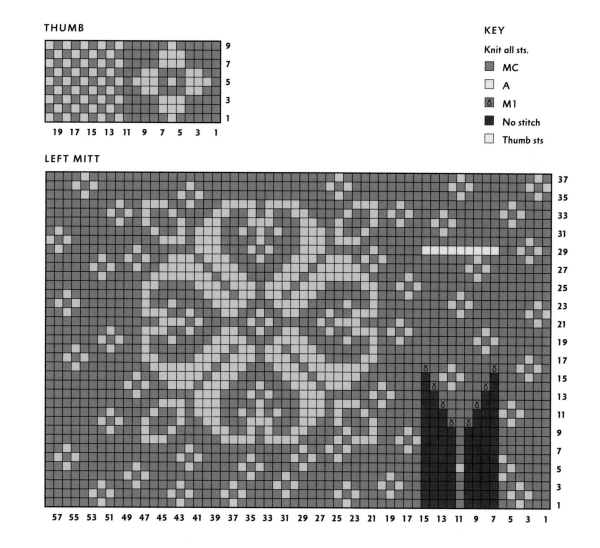

THUMB

9 7 5 3 1

19 17 15 13 11 9 7 5 3 1

KEY

Knit all sts.

▦ MC

☐ A

⊗ M1

■ No stitch

☐ Thumb sts

LEFT MITT

37 35 33 31 29 27 25 23 21 19 17 15 13 11 9 7 5 3 1

57 55 53 51 49 47 45 43 41 39 37 35 33 31 29 27 25 23 21 19 17 15 13 11 9 7 5 3 1

ROSE & CROSS PULLOVER

BY KRISTIN SPURKLAND

Kristin Spurkland drew on traditional Norwegian rose and cross motifs to create this pullover (shown here and on page 139). The main colors of dusky rose and brown are contemporary, but the dashes of true red are classic Norwegian.

SIZES
40 (44, 48)" bust

YARN
Rowan Felted Tweed DK (50% merino wool / 25% alpaca / 25% viscose; 175 yards / 50 grams):
9 (10, 12) balls #148 Sigh (MC); 1 ball #145 Treacle (A); 1 (2, 2) balls #156 Wheat (B); 1 ball #150 Rage (C)

NEEDLES
One 24" (60 cm) long or longer circular (circ) needle size US 3 (3.25 mm)

One 24" (60 cm) long or longer circular needle size US 4 (3.5 mm)

One 24" (60 cm) long or longer circular needle size US 5 (3.75 mm)

One 16" (40 cm) long circular needle size US 4 (3.5 mm)

One set of five double-pointed needles (dpn) size US 4 (3.5 mm)

One set of five double-pointed needles size US 5 (3.75 mm)

NOTIONS
Stitch markers; stitch holder

GAUGE
26 sts and 34 rnds = 4" (10 cm) in Stockinette stitch (St st), using size US 4 needles

26 sts and 28 rnds = 4" (10 cm) in Fair Isle Pattern from Chart D, using size US 5 needles

STITCH PATTERNS

Seeded Rib (multiple of 3 sts; 2-rnd repeat)

Rnd 1: *K2, p1; repeat from * to end.

Rnd 2: K1, *p1, k2; repeat from * to last 2 sts, p1, k1.

Repeat Rnds 1 and 2 for Seeded Rib.

YOKE

Note: Piece is worked from the top down.

Using 16" long size US 4 circ needle and MC, CO 114 (120, 126) sts. Join for working in the rnd, being careful not to twist sts; pm for beginning of rnd. Begin Seeded Rib; work even for 1". Knit 1 rnd.

Shape Yoke
Increase Rnd 1: *K3, M1; repeat from * to end—152 (160, 168) sts.

Next Rnd: Change to 24" long size US 5 circ needle. Begin Fair Isle pattern from Chart A; work Rnds 1-9 once.

Increase Rnd 2: Change to MC. *K4, M1; repeat from * to end—190 (200, 210) sts.

Next Rnd: Begin Fair Isle pattern from Chart B; work Rnds 1-11 once.

Increase Rnd 3: Change to MC. *[K4, M1] 4 (12, 8) times, k3 (2, 3), M1; repeat from * to end—240 (252, 264) sts.

Next Rnd: Begin Fair Isle pattern from Chart C; work Rnds 1-13 once.

SIZE SMALL ONLY
Increase Rnd 4: Change to MC. *K4, M1; repeat from * to end—300 sts.

SIZES MEDIUM AND LARGE ONLY
Increase Rnd 4: Change to MC. *[K4, M1] (4, 3) times, [k5, M1] (1, 2) time(s); repeat from * to end—(312, 324) sts.

ALL SIZES
Next Rnd: Begin Fair Isle pattern from Chart D; work Rnds 1-13 once.

Increase Rnd 5: Change to MC. *[K6, M1] 12 (11, 13) times, [K3 (4, 3), M1] 1 (3, 1) time(s); repeat from * to end—352 (368, 380) sts.

Next Rnd: Begin Fair Isle pattern from Chart A; work Rnds 1-9 once. Change to size US 4 24" circ needle and MC; knit 1 rnd.

SIZES SMALL AND MEDIUM ONLY
Increase Rnd 6: *K8, M1; repeat from * to end—396 (414) sts.

SIZE LARGE ONLY
Increase Rnd 6: *K8, M1; repeat from * to last 4 sts, k4, M1—428 sts.

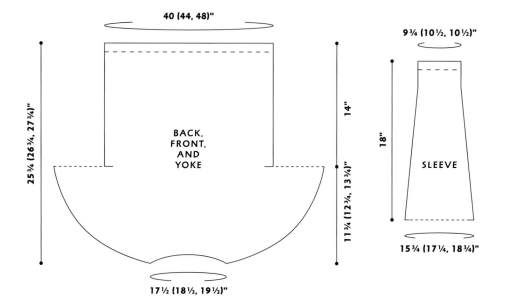

40 (44, 48)"

25 ¾ (26 ¾, 27 ¾)"

BACK, FRONT, AND YOKE

11 ¾ (12 ¾, 13 ¾)"

17 ½ (18 ½, 19 ½)"

9 ¾ (10 ½, 10 ½)"

14"

18"

SLEEVE

15 ¾ (17 ¼, 18 ¾)"

Note: Pieces are worked from the top down.

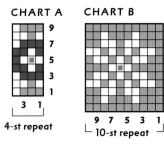

CHART A

9
7
5
3
1

3 1

4-st repeat

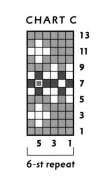

CHART B

11
9
7
5
3
1

9 7 5 3 1

10-st repeat

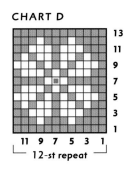

CHART C

13
11
9
7
5
3
1

5 3 1

6-st repeat

CHART D

13
11
9
7
5
3
1

11 9 7 5 3 1

12-st repeat

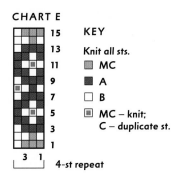

CHART E

15
13
11
9
7
5
3
1

3 1

4-st repeat

KEY

Knit all sts.

▨ MC

■ A

□ B

▣ MC – knit;
   C – duplicate st.

ALL SIZES

Next Rnd: K57 (60, 62) for Back, pm, k84 (88, 90) for Left Sleeve, pm, k114 (119, 124) for Front, pm, k84 (88, 90) for Right Sleeve, pm, knit to end for Back.

Increase Rnd 7: [Knit to 1 st before marker, M1, k2, M1] 4 times, knit to end—404 (422, 436) sts. Knit 1 rnd.

Repeat Increase Rnd 7 every other rnd 4 (8, 12) times—436 (486, 532) sts. Knit 1 rnd.

SIZE SMALL ONLY

Increase Rnd 8: [Knit to marker, sm, k1, M1, knit to 1 st before marker, M1, k1, sm] twice, knit to end—440 sts. Knit 1 rnd.

ALL SIZES

BODY

Divide Body and Sleeves
Next Rnd: K62 (69, 75), place next 96 (106, 116) sts on holder for Left Sleeve, removing markers,

CO 6 sts for underarm, k124 (137, 150), place next 96 (106, 116) sts on holder for Right Sleeve, removing markers, CO 6 sts for underarm, k62 (68, 75)—260 (286, 312) sts. Begin St st (knit every rnd); work even until piece measures 13" from underarm, decrease 2 (1, 0) st(s) on last round—258 (285, 312) sts remain.

Next Rnd: Change to size US 3 circ needle and Seeded Rib; work even for 1". BO all sts in pattern.

SLEEVES

Transfer Sleeve sts to 16" long size US 4 circ needle. With RS facing, rejoin yarn at armhole, pick up and knit 3 sts from sts CO for underarm, pm for beginning of rnd, pick up and knit 3 sts, knit to end—102 (112, 122) sts. Knit 10 (14, 10) rnds.

Shape Sleeve
Note: Change to size US 4 dpns when necessary.

Decrease Rnd: Decrease 2 sts this rnd, then every 6 (5, 4) rnds 18 (21, 26) times, as follows: K1, ssk, knit to last 3 sts, k2tog, k1—64 (68, 68) sts. Work even until piece measures 15" from underarm.

Next Rnd: Change to larger dpns. Begin Fair Isle pattern from Chart E; work Rnds 1-15 once.

Next Rnd: Change to smaller dpns. Knit 1 rnd, decrease 1 (2, 2) sts—63 (66, 66) sts remain.

Next Rnd: Change to Seeded Rib; work even for 1". BO all sts in pattern.

FINISHING

Using C, work duplicate st (see Special Techniques, page 000) as indicated in all Charts. Block as desired.

MINERVA BONNET

BY TEVA DURHAM

Somewhere between a slouchy beret and a milkmaid's bonnet, this hat (see left and page 140) was inspired by one created and worn by Teva Durham's grandmother Minerva. Its shape and design reminded Minerva of the citizen's bonnet of the French Revolution, and she once wrote that the hat was like one worn "by poor Marie Antoinette on her way to the scaffold." Teva hopes that her remake will be worn on far more pleasant outings.

FINISHED MEASUREMENTS

22 ½" circumference at Brim

Note: Fit of Brim may be adjusted once Hat is complete.

YARN

Loop-d-Loop by Teva Durham Moss (85% extrafine merino wool / 15% nylon; 163 yards / 50 grams): 2 balls #01 Cream

NEEDLES

One set of five double-pointed needles (dpn) size US 4 (3.5 mm)

One 16" (40 cm) circular (circ) needle size US 4 (3.5 mm)

One 16" (40 cm) circular needle size US 7 (4.5 mm)

Change needle size if necessary to obtain correct gauge.

NOTIONS

Stitch marker; 1 yard ⅝-1" wide hem tape, bias tape, or ribbon; sewing needle and thread to match

GAUGE

20 sts and 28 rows = 4" (10cm) over Crown Chart Rows 15-26, using smaller needle

18 sts and 24 rows = 4" (10cm) over Crown Chart Rows 15-26, using larger needle

NOTE

The Hat is worked in-the-round from the top down, and finished with a Corded Bind-Off edge.

CROWN

Using dpns, CO 6 sts onto each of 3 dpns, as follows: Make a slip knot and place it on dpn. *With empty dpn, [pick up and knit 1 st from loop, yo] 3 times; repeat from * twice, using new dpn each time. Remove original dpn holding the loop—18 sts (6 sts each dpn). Join for working in the rnd; pm for beginning of rnd.

Next Rnd: *K1-f/b, k2; repeat from * to end—24 sts. Knit 1 rnd. Redistribute sts evenly among 4 dpns.

Shape Crown

Note: Change to circ needle when desired for number of sts on needles.

CROWN CHART

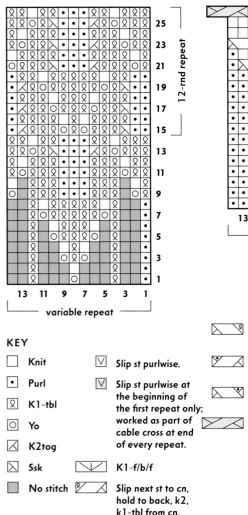

13 11 9 7 5 3 1

variable repeat

Next Rnd: Begin Crown Chart; work Rnds 1-26 once. Change to larger needle; work Rnds 15-26 twice.

BRIM CHART

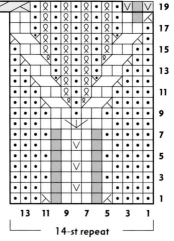

13 11 9 7 5 3 1

14-st repeat

KEY

☐ Knit		� Slip st purlwise.	
• Purl		Slip st purlwise at the beginning of the first repeat only; worked as part of cable cross at end of every repeat.	
⍉ K1-tbl			
○ Yo			
⟋ K2tog			
⟍ Ssk		K1-f/b/f	
▨ No stitch		Slip next st to cn, hold to back, k2, k1-tbl from cn.	

Slip 2 sts to cn, hold to front, k1-tbl, k2 from cn.

Slip next st to cn, hold to back, k2, p1 from cn.

Slip 2 sts to cn, hold to front, p1, k2 from cn.

Slip 2 sts to cn, hold to back, k2, k2 from cn. Worked over the last 2 sts of the repeat and the first 2 sts of the next repeat; the last repeat is worked over the last 2 sts of the rnd and the first 2 sts of the next rnd.

BRIM

Next Rnd: Change to smaller circ needle and Brim Chart; work Rnds 1-19 once—104 sts remain.

Corded BO Row: Slip last 2 sts worked to dpn, k1 from circ needle, pass next-to-last st over last st, turn, p2, turn. *K2 on dpn, k1 from circ needle, pass next-to-last st over last st, turn, p2, turn; repeat from * until 9 sts have been bound-off (sts 4-12 of Brim Chart). Cut yarn, leaving 8" tail. Using Kitchener st (see Special Techniques, page 000), graft 2 remaining sts on dpn to next 2 sts on circ needle, creating a continuous arched knit column. **Slip next 2 sts to dpn, rejoin yarn, k1 from circ needle, pass next-to-last st over last st, turn, p2, turn. *K2 on dpn, k1 from circ needle, pass next-to-last st over last st, turn, p2, turn; repeat from * until 9 sts have been bound-off. Cut yarn, leaving 8" tail. Graft 2 remaining sts on dpn to next 2 sts on circ needle. Repeat from ** until all sts have been BO.

FINISHING

Block as desired. Try on for fit. Using sewing needle and thread, sew one edge of hem tape, bias tape or ribbon to WS, at beginning of Brim (Rnd 1 of Chart C), adjusting length of tape or ribbon to fit snugly around head. Sew remaining edge of tape or ribbon; sew ends together.

TILDEN BABY HAT

BY JARED FLOOD

Once deep into the "culture of art for art's sake," designer Jared Flood ultimately realized that, like his parents, his creativity flourishes when he is able to meld beauty and utility. Jared named this colorwork hat after the place that inspired it: the beaches of Fort Tilden in Queens, New York, where sand dunes and sea contrast with forgotten metal and concrete leftover from its days as a military base.

SIZES
To fit average child's head

FINISHED MEASUREMENTS
18" circumference

YARN
Jamieson's Spindrift (100% Shetland wool; 125 yards / 25 grams): 1 ball each #1190 Burnt Umber (A) and #1160 Scotch Broom (B)

NEEDLES
One 16" (40 cm) long circular (circ) needle size US 2 (2.75 mm)

One 16" (40 cm) long circular needle size US 5 (3.75 mm)

One set of five double-pointed needles size US 5 (3.75 mm)

Change needle size if necessary to obtain correct gauge.

NOTIONS
Stitch marker

GAUGE
28 sts and 28 rnds = 4" (10 cm) in Fair Isle Pattern from Chart, using larger needle

STITCH PATTERN
2x2 Rib (multiple of 4 sts; 1-rnd repeat)

All Rnds: *K2, p2; repeat from * to end.

HAT
BRIM
Using smaller needle and A, CO 116 sts. Join for working in the rnd, being careful not to twist sts; place marker (pm) for beginning of rnd. Begin 2x2 Rib; work even until piece measures just under 1" from the beginning.

Next Rnd: *K11, M1; repeat from * to last 6 sts, knit to end—126 sts. Knit 1 rnd. Change to B; knit 1 rnd.

CROWN
Next Rnd: Change to Fair Isle Pattern from Chart on page 107; work even until Chart is complete, working decreases as indicated in Chart— 18 sts remain. Cut yarns, leaving 8" tails. Thread tails through remaining sts, pull tight, and fasten off.

FINISHING
Wet or steam block, making sure that shaping lies flat.

FAIR ISLE PATTERN FOR TILDEN

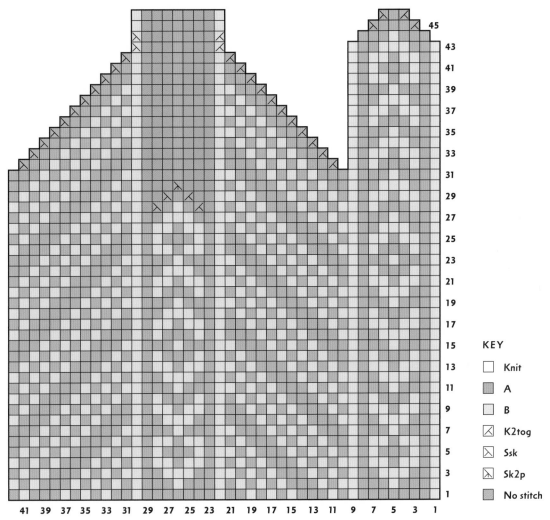

KEY

- ☐ Knit
- ▨ A
- ☐ B
- ⍂ K2tog
- ⍁ Ssk
- ⍍ Sk2p
- ▨ No stitch

CROCUS PATCH BABY BLANKET

BY ANNE HANSON

Anne Hanson's grandmother probably made more than a hundred afghans in her lifetime. This lace blanket is Anne's delicate contribution to her legacy. The crocus pattern keeps knitters engaged and babies warm and cozy. The pattern includes three sizes—to fit in a stroller or car seat, crib, or larger bed.

SIZES
Carriage (small crib square, large crib square)

FINISHED MEASUREMENTS
30½ (40¾, 44¾)" wide by 36¾ (40¾, 44¾)" long, after blocking

YARN
Pico Accuardi Dyeworks Marco Bambino (100% superwash merino wool; 380 yards / 100 grams): 3 (4, 5) hanks Redwood

NEEDLES
One 24" (60 cm) long circular (circ) needle size US 4 (3.5 mm)

Change needle size if necessary to obtain correct gauge.

NOTIONS
Stitch markers (optional)

GAUGE
21 sts and 32 rows = 4" (10 cm) in Crocus Lace, after blocking

24 sts and 32 rows = 4" (10 cm) in Stockinette stitch (St st)

STITCH PATTERN

Crocus Lace (multiple of 24 sts + 19; 32-row repeat) (see Chart)

Row 1 (RS): K9, *p1, yo, k2, ssk, p5, k2tog, yo, p1, yo, ssk, p5, k2tog, k2, yo; repeat from * to last 10 sts, p1, knit to end.

Row 2: K10, *p4, k5, p2, k1, p2, k5, p4, k1; repeat from * to last 9 sts, knit to end.

Row 3: K9, *p1, k1, yo, k2, ssk, p4, yo, ssk, p1, k2tog, yo, p4, k2tog, k2, yo, k1; repeat from * to last 10 sts, p1, knit to end.

Row 4: K10, *p5, k4, p2, k1, p2, k4, p5, k1; repeat from * to last 9 sts, knit to end.

Row 5: K9, *p1, k2, yo, k2, ssk, p3, k2tog, yo, p1, yo, ssk, p3, k2tog, k2, yo, k2; repeat from * to last 10 sts, p1, knit to end.

Row 6: K10, *p6, k3, p2, k1, p2, k3, p6, k1; repeat from * to last 9 sts, knit to end.

Row 7: K9, *p1, k3, yo, k2, ssk, p2, yo, ssk, p1, k2tog, yo, p2, k2tog, k2, yo, k3; repeat from * to last 10 sts, p1, knit to end.

Rows 8, 10, and 12: K10, *p7, k2, p2, k1, p2, k2, p7, k1; repeat from * to last 9 sts, knit to end.

Row 9: K9, *p1, yo, k2, ssk, k3, p2, k2tog, yo, p1, yo, ssk, p2, k3, k2tog, k2, yo; repeat from * to last 10 sts, p1, knit to end.

Row 11: K9, *p1, k1, yo, k2, ssk, k2, p2, yo, ssk, p1, k2tog, yo, p2, k2, k2tog, k2, yo, k1; repeat from * to last 10 sts, p1, knit to end.

Row 13: K9, *p1, [yo, ssk] twice, k1, k2tog, yo, p2, k2tog, yo, p1, yo, ssk, p2, yo, ssk, k1, [k2tog, yo] twice; repeat from * to last 10 sts, p1, knit to end.

Row 14: K10, *p6, k3, p2, k1, p2, k3, p6, k1; repeat from * to last 9 sts, knit to end.

Row 15: K9, *p1, k2tog, yo, p1, yo, k3tog, yo, p2, k2tog, yo, k1, p1, k1, yo, ssk, p2, yo, sk2p, yo, p1, yo, ssk; repeat from * to last 10 sts, p1, knit to end.

Row 16: K10, *p2, k2, p1, k3, p3, k1, p3, k3, p1, k2, p2, k1; repeat from * to last 9 sts, knit to end.

Row 17: K9, *p1, yo, ssk, p5, k2tog, k2, yo, p1, yo, k2, ssk, p5, k2tog, yo; repeat from * to last 10 sts, p1, knit to end.

Row 18: K10, *p2, k5, p4, k1, p4, k5, p2, k1; repeat from * to last 9 sts, knit to end.

Row 19: K9, *p1, k2tog, yo, p4, k2tog, k2, yo, k1, p1, k1, yo, k2, ssk, p4, yo, ssk; repeat from * to last 10 sts, p1, knit to end.

Row 20: K10, *p2, k4, p5, k1, p5, k4, p2, k1; repeat from * to last 9 sts, knit to end.

Row 21: K9, *p1, yo, ssk, p3, k2tog, k2, yo, k2, p1, k2, yo, k2, ssk, p3, k2tog, yo; repeat from * to last 10 sts, p1, knit to end.

Row 22: K10, *p2, k3, p6, k1, p6, k3, p2, k1; repeat from * to last 9 sts, knit to end.

Row 23: K9, *p1, k2tog, yo, p2, k2tog, k2, yo, k3, p1, k3, yo, k2, ssk, p2, yo, ssk; repeat from * to last 10 sts, p1, knit to end.

Rows 24, 26, and 28: K10, *p2, k2, p7, k1, p7, k2, p2, k1; repeat from * to last 9 sts, knit to end.

Row 25: K9, *p1, yo, ssk, p2, k3, k2tog, k2, yo, p1, yo, k2, ssk, k3, p2, k2tog, yo; repeat from * to last 10 sts, p1, knit to end.

Row 27: K9, *p1, k2tog, yo, p2, k2, k2tog, k2, yo, k1, p1, k1, yo, k2, ssk, k2, p2, yo, ssk; repeat from * to last 9 sts, p1, knit to end.

Row 29: K9, *p1, yo, ssk, p2, yo, ssk, k1, [k2tog, yo] twice, p1, [yo, ssk] twice, k1, k2tog, yo, p2, k2tog, yo; repeat from * to last 10 sts, p1, knit to end.

Row 30: K10, *p2, k3, p6, k1, p6, k3, p2, k1; repeat from * to last 9 sts, knit to end.

Row 31: K9, *p1, k1, yo, ssk, p2, yo, sk2p, yo, p1, yo, ssk, p1, k2tog, yo, p1, yo, k3tog, yo, p2, k2tog, yo, k1; repeat from * to last 10 sts, p1, knit to end.

Row 32: K10, *p3, k3, p1, k2, p2, k1, p2, k2, p1, k3, p3, k1; repeat from * to last 9 sts, knit to end.

Repeat Rows 1-32 for Crocus Lace.

BLANKET

CO 163 (211, 235) sts. Knit 16 rows.

Set-Up Row 1 (RS): K9, place marker (pm) (optional), *p1, k1, yo, ssk, p6, yo, ssk, p1, k2tog, yo, p6, k2tog, yo, k1; repeat from * to last 10 sts, pm (optional), p1, knit to end.

Set-Up Row 2: K10, *p3, k6, p2, k1, p2, k6, p3, k1; repeat from * to last 9 sts, knit to end.

Next Row: Begin Crocus Lace from pattern text or Chart; work Rows 1-32 eight (9, 10) times, then repeat Rows 1-14 once more.

Next Row: K9, *p1, k2tog, yo, p1, yo, k3tog, yo, p3, yo, ssk, p1, k2tog, yo, p3, yo, sk2p, yo, p1, yo, ssk; repeat from * to last 10 sts, p1, knit to end.

Next Row: K10, *p2, k2, p1, k4, p2, k1, p2, k4, p1, k2, p2, k1; repeat from * to last 9 sts, knit to end.

Knit 16 rows. BO all sts knitwise.

FINISHING

Block to measurements.

CROCUS LACE

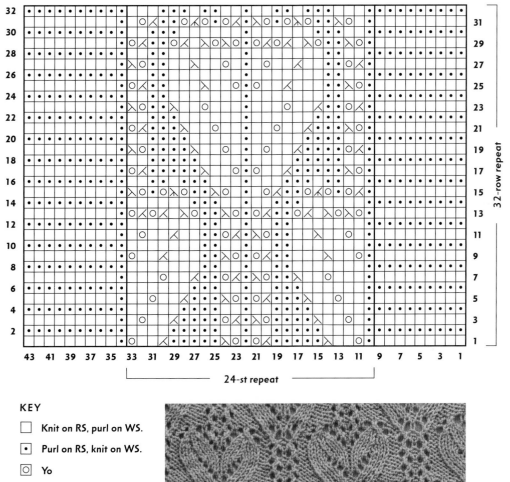

KEY

- ☐ Knit on RS, purl on WS.
- • Purl on RS, knit on WS.
- ◯ Yo
- ╱ K2tog
- ╲ Ssk
- ⋏ Sk2p
- ◿ K3tog

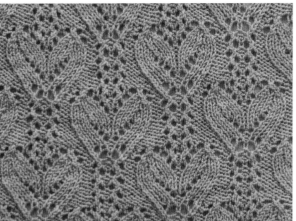

111

CONOVER MITTENS

BY DAVID CASTILLO

David Castillo was thinking of his grandfather, Robert Conover—a graphic designer and photographer in the midcentury modern period in San Francisco—when he designed these mittens. David suspects that Grandpa would have appreciated their balance, line, and functional artistry.

SIZES
Small (Medium, Large)

To fit child (large child/woman/ small man, large woman/man)

FINISHED MEASUREMENTS
7 ¼ (8, 8 ¾)" circumference

YARN
Cascade Yarns Greenland (100% superwash merino; 137 yards / 100 grams): 1 hank each A and B; Shown in Small: #3527 Sunflower (A) and #3532 Lemon Yellow (B); Large: #3533 Tan (A) and #3518 Blue Hawaii (B)

NEEDLES
One set of five double-pointed needles (dpn) size US 7 (4.5 mm)

Change needle size if necessary to obtain correct gauge.

NOTIONS
Stitch markers, including removable stitch marker

GAUGE
20 sts and 28 rnds = 4" (10 cm) in Stockinette stitch (St st) (knit every rnd)

STITCH PATTERNS

Stripe Pattern
*Work [1 rnd B, 3 rnds A] twice, 3 rnds B, 3 rnds A; repeat from * for Stripe Pattern.

2x2 Rib (multiple of 4 sts; 1-rnd repeat)

All Rnds: *K2, p2; repeat from * to end.

NOTE
Mitten One is worked first from the top down, followed by a connecting I-Cord, and then Mitten Two is worked from the bottom up.

MITTEN ONE
THUMB

Using A and Judy's Magic CO (see Special Techniques, page 139), CO 3 (4, 5) sts onto each of 2 needles—6 (8, 10) sts.

Note: All sts CO during shaping (after initial CO) are CO using Backward Loop CO (see Special Techniques, page 000), unless otherwise indicated.

Shape Thumb
Increase Rnd: Needle 1: K1, CO 1 st, knit to last st, CO 1 st, k1; **Needle 2:** K1, CO 1 st, knit to last st, CO 1 st, k1—10 (12, 14) sts. Knit 1 rnd.

Repeat Increase Rnd once—14 (16, 18) sts. Divide sts among 4 needles [3-4-3-4 (4-4-4-4, 4-5-4-5)]. Continuing in St st (knit every rnd), work even until piece measures 2 ¼" from the beginning. Transfer sts to waste yarn; cut yarn and set aside.

MITTEN TOP

Using A and Judy's Magic CO, CO 6 (8, 10) sts onto each of 2 needles—12 (16, 20) sts. Knit 1 rnd. Divide sts evenly among 4 needles [3-3-3-3 (4-4-4-4, 5-5-5-5)].

Shape Mitten Top

Increase Rnd: Needle 1: K1, CO 1 st, knit to end; **Needle 2:** Knit to last st, CO 1 st, k1; **Needle 3:** K1, CO 1 st, knit to end; **Needle 4:** Knit to last st, CO 1 st, k1—16 (20, 24) sts. Knit 1 rnd.

Repeat Increase Rnd every other rnd 5 times—36 (40, 44) sts [9-9-9-9 (10-10-10-10, 11-11-11-11)].

HAND

Next Rnd: Change to St st and Stripe Pattern; work even until piece measures 5 ½" from the beginning.

Join Thumb

Next Rnd: Transfer sts from Needle 2 to Needle 1 and sts from Needle 4 to Needle 3; these are now Needles 1 and 2. Transfer Thumb sts from waste yarn to 2 needles (Needles 3 and 4). **Needle 1:** Continuing in Stripe Pattern, knit; **Needle 2:** Knit to last st, pm, ssk (1 st from Needle 2 together with 1 st from Needle 3); **Needle 3:** Knit; **Needle 4:** Knit to last st, k2tog (1 st from Needle 4 together with 1 st from Needle 1, pm, knit to end of Needle 1; pm for new beginning of rnd—48 (54, 60) sts. Redistribute sts among needles [12-12-12-12 (13-14-13-14, 15-15-15-15)]. Knit 2 rnds.

THUMB GUSSET

Decrease Rnd: Needle 1: Continuing in Stripe Pattern, knit; **Needle 2:** Knit to marker, ssk, knit to end; **Needle 3:** Knit to 2 sts before marker, k2tog, knit to end; **Needle 4:** Knit—46 (52, 58) sts remain. Knit 2 rnds.

Repeat Decrease Rnd every 3 rnds 4 (5, 6) times, then every other rnd once, removing Thumb Gusset markers on last rnd—36 (40, 44) sts remain.

CUFF

Next Rnd: Continuing in Stripe Pattern, change to 2x2 Rib; work even for 15 rnds. Change to B; knit 1 rnd.

BO Rnd: Using Cable CO (see Special Techniques, page 000), CO 3 sts. K2, ssk. Do not turn. *Slide sts back to right-hand end of needle; k2, ssk, pulling yarn from right to left for first st. Repeat from * until 4 sts remain. Work I-Cord (see Special Techniques, page 138) on remaining 4 sts for approximately 2'. Change to A and continue in I-Cord for approximately 2' more. Place removable marker on first st.

MITTEN TWO

CUFF

Work 36 (40, 44) more rows of I-Cord. BO all sts. Beginning at BO edge, pick up and knit 1 st for each row of I-Cord to marker, picking up st through half of I-Cord st column—36 (40, 44) sts. Remove marker. Divide sts evenly among 4 needles. Join for working in the rnd; pm for beginning of rnd. Begin 2x2 Rib and Stripe Pattern, matching stripes as worked on Mitten One, but reversing colors, working A instead of B, and vice versa; work even for 15 rows.

THUMB GUSSET

Increase Rnd: Needle 1: Knit; **Needle 2:** Knit to end, pm, LLI; **Needle 3:** RLI, pm, knit to end; **Needle 4:** Knit—38 (42, 46) sts. Knit 1 rnd.

Repeat Increase Rnd every 3 rnds 6 (7, 8) times—50 (56, 62) sts.

Next Rnd: Knit to marker, transfer next 14 (16, 18) sts to waste yarn for Thumb, removing markers, knit to end—36 (40, 44) sts [9-9-9-9 (10-10-10-10, 11-11-11-11)].

HAND

Next Rnd: Continuing with Stripe Pattern, work even until Hand measures same as for Mitten One from end of Thumb Gusset to beginning of Mitten Top shaping.

MITTEN TOP

Shape Mitten Top
Decrease Rnd: Needle 1: Ssk, knit to end; **Needle 2:** Knit to last 2 sts, k2tog; **Needle 3:** Ssk, knit to end; **Needle 4:** Knit to last 2 sts, k2tog—32 (36, 40) sts remain. Knit 1 rnd.

Repeat Decrease Rnd every other rnd 5 times—12 (16, 20) sts remain. Cut yarn, leaving long tail. Transfer sts from Needle 1 to Needle 4 and sts from Needle 3 to Needle 2. Using Kitchener st (see Special Techniques, page 000), graft sts.

THUMB

Transfer sts from waste yarn to 4 dpns [3-4-3-4 (4-4-4-4, 4-5-4-5)]. Rejoin B. Begin St st; work even until piece measures same as for Mitten One from end of Thumb Gusset to beginning of Thumb shaping.

Shape Thumb
Work Decrease Rnd as for Mitten Top every other rnd twice—6 (8, 10) sts remain. Cut yarn, leaving long tail. Complete as for Mitten Top.

FINISHING

Using yarn tails, sew gap between Hand and Thumb Gusset. Block as desired.

EDNA SLOUCH HAT

BY LEIGH RADFORD

Leigh Radford's grandmother was a seamstress and made petticoats, layering Leigh with yards of tulle underneath skirts of dotted swiss. But her auntie Edna made her much less girly gear, including a new striped and pom-pommed stocking cap each summer, for camping in the chilly Pacific Northwest. Leigh used scraps of thick-and-thin yarn to create a slouchy, updated version.

FINISHED MEASUREMENTS

18 ¼" circumference

YARN

Manos del Uruguay Wool Clasica (100% wool; 135 yards / 100 grams): 1 hank each #E English (MC), #69 Hibiscus (A), and #40 Goldenrod (B).

NEEDLES

One 16" long circular (circ) needle size US 10 (6 mm)

One set of five double-pointed needles (dpn) size US 10 (6 mm)

Change needle size if necessary to obtain correct gauge.

NOTIONS

Stitch marker

GAUGE

15 sts and 21 rows = 4" (10 cm)

STITCH PATTERN

Twisted Rib (multiple of 2 sts; 1-rnd repeat)

All Rnds: *K1-tbl, p1; repeat from * to end.

BRIM

Using MC, CO 72 sts. Join for working in the rnd, being careful not to twist sts; pm for beginning of rnd. Begin Twisted Rib; work even until piece measures 2 ¾" from CO.

CROWN

Next Rnd: Change to St st. Work 3 rnds A, 2 rnds B, 2 rnds MC, then 3 rnds A. Change to MC; work even until piece measures 6 ½" from CO.

Shape Crown

Next Rnd: *K12, M1; repeat from * to end—78 sts. Work even until piece measures 9 ½" from CO. Place marker after st 39.

Shape Top

Note: Change to dpns when necessary for number of sts on needle.

Dec Rnd 1: Decrease 8 sts this rnd, then every other rnd 4 times, as follows: *K1, [ssk] twice, knit to 5 sts before next marker, [k2tog] twice, k1; repeat from * to end—38 sts remain. Knit 1 rnd.

Dec Rnd 2: *K1, [ssk] 3 times, knit to 7 sts before next marker, [k2tog] 3 times, k1; repeat from * to end—26 sts remain. Cut yarn, leaving 18" long tail. Divide sts evenly between 2 needles. Graft sts using Kitchener st (see Special Techniques, page 139).

FINISHING

Block as desired. Make 3 ½" pom pom (see Special Techniques, page 140) and sew to center top of Hat.

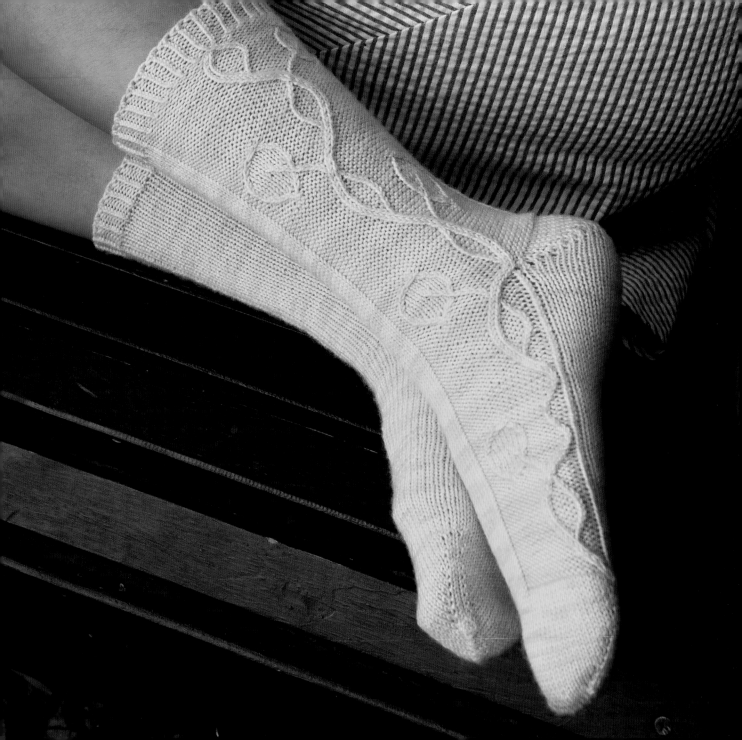

'OLINA SOCKS

BY EMILY JOHNSON

Emily Johnson designed these stunning socks in honor of the land where her great-grandparents lived. The Morines—Jessie and Charles Victor—ventured to Hawaii in the 1920s. The floral cables recall the leis of plumeria that are abundant there. 'Olina means "to make merry," and these socks are a joyous celebration of Emily's family ties.

FINISHED MEASUREMENTS
9 ½" Foot length from back of Heel
8 ½" Foot circumference
8" Leg length from base of Heel

YARN
Shibui Knits Sock (100% superwash merino wool; 191 yards / 50 grams): 2 hanks Blossom

NEEDLES
One set of five double-pointed needles (dpn) size US 1 (2.25 mm)
One set of five double-pointed needles size US 2 (2.75 mm)
Change needle size if necessary to obtain correct gauge.

NOTIONS
Stitch markers; cable needle (cn) (optional)

GAUGE
32 sts and 48 rnds = 4" (10 cm) in Stockinette stitch (St st), using smaller needles

ABBREVIATIONS
T2R: Slip next st to cn, hold to back, k1-tbl, k1-tbl from cn. To work without a cn, with right-hand needle at front of work, skip first st on left-hand needle, insert right-hand needle into front of second st purlwise and slip both sts from left-hand needle; with left-hand needle, pick up hanging first st from behind right-hand needle, slip st from right-hand needle back to left-hand needle, [k1-tbl] twice.

T2L: Slip next st to cn, hold to front, k1-tbl, k1-tbl from cn. To work without a cn, with right-hand needle at back of work, skip first st on left-hand needle, insert right-hand needle into back of second st purlwise and slip both sts from left-hand needle; with left needle, pick up hanging first st from in front of right needle, slip st from right needle back to left needle, [k1-tbl] twice.

T2R-p: Slip next st to cn, hold to back, k1-tbl, p1 from cn. To work without a cn, with right-hand needle at front of work, skip first st on left-hand needle, insert right-hand needle into front of second st purlwise and slip both sts from left-hand needle; with left-hand needle, pick up hanging first st from behind right-hand needle, slip st from right-hand needle back to left-hand needle, k1-tbl, p1.

T2L-p: Slip next st to cn, hold to front, p1, k1-tbl from cn. To work without a cn, with right-hand needle at back of work, skip first st on left-hand needle, insert right-hand needle into back of second st purlwise and slip both sts from left-hand needle; with left-hand needle, pick up hanging first st from in front of right-hand needle, slip st from right-hand needle back to left-hand needle, p1, k1-tbl.

1/2 LPC: Slip next st to cn, hold to front, k1-tbl, p1, k1-tbl from cn. To work without a cn, with right-hand needle at back of work, skip first st on left-hand needle, insert right-hand needle into back of second and third sts and slip all 3 sts from left-hand needle; with left-hand needle, pick up hanging st from in front of right-hand needle, k1-tbl, p1, k1-tbl.

2/1 LC: Slip 2 sts to cn, hold to front, k1-tbl, k2 from cn. To work without a cn, with right-hand needle at back of work, skip first 2 sts on left-hand needle, insert right-hand needle into back of third st purlwise and slip all 3 sts from left-hand needle; with left-hand needle, pick up hanging sts from in front of right-hand needle, slip st from right-hand needle back to left-hand needle, [k1-tbl] 3 times.

2/1 RC: Slip next st to cn, hold to back, [k1-tbl] twice, k1-tbl from cn. To work without a cn, with right-hand needle at front of work, skip first st on left-hand needle, insert right-hand needle into front of second and third sts purlwise and slip all 3 sts from left-hand needle; with left-hand needle, pick up hanging st from in back of right-hand needle, slip st from right-hand needle back to left-hand needle, [k1-tbl] 3 times.

2/1 LPC: Slip 2 sts to cn, hold to front, p1, [k1-tbl] twice from cn. To work without a cn, with right-hand needle at back of work, skip first 2 sts on left-hand needle, insert right-hand needle into back of third st and slip all 3 sts from left-hand needle; with left-hand needle, pick up hanging sts from in front of right-hand needle, slip st from right-hand needle back to left-hand needle, p1, [k1-tbl] twice from cn.

2/1 RPC: Slip next st to cn, hold to back, [k1-tbl] twice, p1 from cn. To work without a cn, with right-hand needle at front of work, skip first st on left-hand needle, insert right-hand needle into second and third sts purlwise and slip all 3 sts from left-hand needle; with left-hand needle, pick up hanging st from in back of right-hand needle, slip sts from right-hand needle back to left-hand needle, [k1-tbl] twice, p1.

3/1 LPC: Slip next st to cn, hold to front, p3, p1 from cn. To work without a cn, with right-hand needle at back of work, skip first st on left-hand needle, insert right-hand needle into back of second, third, and fourth sts and slip all 4 sts from left-hand needle; with left-hand needle, pick up hanging st from in front of right-hand needle, p4.

3/1 RPC: Slip next st to cn, hold to front, p3, then p1 from cn. To work without a cn, with right-hand needle at front of work, skip first 3 sts on left-hand needle, insert right-hand needle into fourth st purlwise and slip all 4 sts from left-hand needle; with left-hand needle, pick up hanging sts from in back of right-hand needle, p4.

STITCH PATTERN

Twisted Rib (multiple of 2 sts; 1-rnd repeat)

All Rnds: *K1-tbl, p1; repeat from * to end.

LEFT SOCK

TOE

Using Judy's Magic CO (see Special Techniques, page 000), CO 12 sts onto each of 2 needles—24 sts. Knit 1 rnd. Divide sts evenly among 4 needles [6-6-6-6]; pm for beginning of rnd.

Shape Toe

Increase Rnd: Needle 1: *K1, M1, knit to end; **Needle 2:** Knit to last st, M1, k1; **Needle 3:** *K1, M1, knit to end; **Needle 4:** Knit to last st, M1, k1—28 sts. Knit 1 rnd.

Repeat Increase Rnd every other rnd 7 times, then every 4 rnds twice—64 sts [16-16-16-16].

FOOT

Next Rnd: Needle 1: K32; **Needle 2:** K15; **Needle 3:** K15; pm for new beginning of rnd, transfer last 2 sts on Needle 3 to Needle 1 [34-15-15].

Next Rnd: Needle 1: K1, k1-tbl, work across 18 sts from Left Foot Chart, knit to end; **Needles 2 and 3:** Knit. Work even until piece measures 7 ½" from the beginning; take note of last Rnd of Chart worked. K2 from Needle 1 onto Needle 3. Turn.

HEEL

Note: Heel is shaped using Short Rows (see Special Techniques, page 000).

Short Rows 1 (WS) and 2 (RS): Working only on 32 sts on Needles 2 and 3, slip 1, p28, wrp-t, k26, wrp-t.

Short Rows 3 and 4: Purl to 1 st before wrapped st from row below previous row, wrp-t; knit to 1 st before wrapped st from row below previous row, wrp-t.

Repeat Short Rows 3 and 4 until 12 sts remain in the center of the Heel.

Short Rows 5 and 6: Purl to first wrapped st from row below previous row, work wrap together with wrapped st, wrp-t; knit to first wrapped st from row below previous row, work wrap together with wrapped st, wrp-t. *Note: You will be wrapping sts that have already been wrapped. When you work the*

LEG CHART

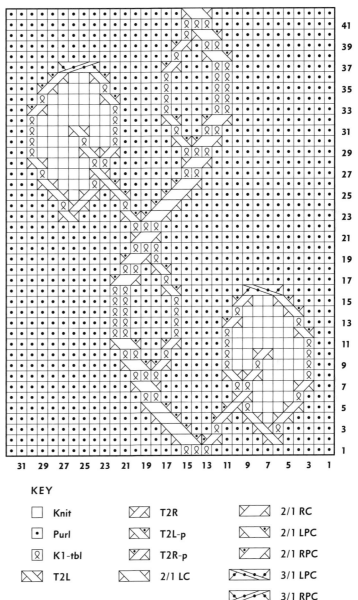

KEY

☐ Knit	◩ T2R	◩ 2/1 RC	
· Purl	◪ T2L-p	◣ 2/1 LPC	
ℚ K1-tbl	◤ T2R-p	◥ 2/1 RPC	
◩ T2L	◣ 2/1 LC	◺ 3/1 LPC	
		◹ 3/1 RPC	

LEFT FOOT CHART

RIGHT FOOT CHART

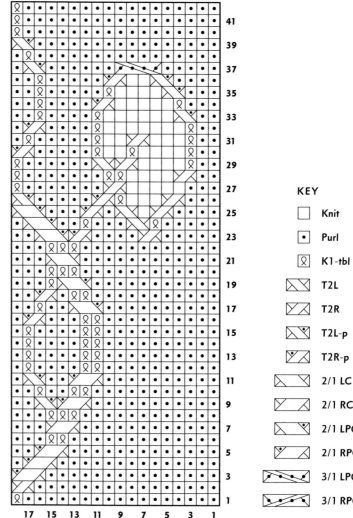

KEY

▢	Knit
•	Purl
ℚ	K1-tbl
⟋	T2L
⟋	T2R
⟋	T2L-p
⟋	T2R-p
⟋	2/1 LC
⟋	2/1 RC
⟋	2/1 LPC
⟋	2/1 RPC
⟋	3/1 LPC
⟋	3/1 RPC

wraps together with the wrapped sts on following rows, make sure to work both wraps together with the wrapped st.

Repeat Short Rows 5 and 6 until 2 sts remain unworked on either side, ending with a WS row. Knit to last 12 Heel sts.

LEG

Note: Work remaining wraps together with wrapped sts as you come to them.

Next Rnd: Rearrange sts as follows: **Needle 1:** K1, k1-tbl, work across 32 sts from Leg Chart, beginning with Rnd number following last Rnd number worked in Left Foot Chart, k2; **Needles 2 and 3:** K14; pm for beginning of rnd—64 sts [36-14-14]. Work even until piece measures 7" from beginning of Leg, ending with Rnd 20 of Leg Chart.

Next Rnd: Needle 1: K1, k1-tbl, p17, 1/2 LPC, p6, M1-p, p6, k2; **Needle 2:** K10, M1, knit to end; **Needle 3:** Knit to end, k1 from Needle 1, pm for new beginning of rnd—66 sts [36-15-15].

CUFF

Next Rnd: Change to larger needles and Twisted Rib; work even until Cuff measures ¾".

BO Rnd: Yrn, k1-tbl, pass yrn over k1-tbl, *yo, p1, pass yo over p1, pass second st over last st, yrn, k1-tbl, pass yrn over k1-tbl, pass second st over last st; repeat from * until 1 st remains. Fasten off.

RIGHT SOCK

Work as for Left Sock to end of Toe shaping—64 sts [16-16-16-16].

FOOT

Next Rnd: Needle 1: K34; **Needle 2:** K15; **Needle 3:** K15; pm for new beginning of rnd [34-15-15].

Next Rnd: Needle 1: K13, k1-tbl, work across 18 sts from Right Foot Chart, k2; **Needles 2 and 3:** Knit. Work even until piece measures 7 ½" from the beginning; take note of last Rnd of Chart worked. K2 from Needle 1 onto Needle 3. Turn.

HEEL

Work short row shaping as for Left Sock, ending with a WS row, k14.

LEG

Note: Work remaining wraps together with wrapped sts as you come to them.

Next Rnd: Rearrange sts as follows: **Needle 1:** K14; **Needle 2:** K14; **Needle 3:** K1, k1-tbl, work across 32 sts from Leg Chart, beginning with Rnd number 20 rnds less than last Rnd number worked in Right Foot Chart (for example, if you ended Right Foot Chart with Rnd 25, begin Leg Chart with Rnd 5), k2; pm for beginning of rnd—64 sts [14-14-36]. Work even until piece measures 7" from beginning of Leg, ending with Rnd 41 of Leg Chart. Knit across Needles 1 and 2.

Next Rnd: Needle 3: K1, k1-tbl, p6, M1-p, p6, 1/2 LPC, p17, k2; **Needle 1:** K10, M1, knit to end; **Needle 2:** Knit to end, k1 from Needle 3; pm for new beginning of rnd—66 sts [36-15-15].

CUFF

Complete as for Left Sock.

FINISHING

Block as desired.

HELEN & WENDY'S SLIPPERS

BY WENDY BERNARD

It seems like every 1970s knitter made some variation on house slippers. In Wendy Bernard's household, they were coveted like crazy. Her grandma Helen was a slow knitter—perhaps because she was paying more attention to Lawrence Welk than her needles—and family members begged to be next in line for a pair. Wendy updates them here with two cozy versions. The gold pair reflects Helen's straightforward style, and the bright turquoise pair shows Wendy's flowery take on the basic form.

SIZES
Youth/Women's Small (Women's Medium, Women's Large/Men's Small, Men's Medium/Large)

FINISHED MEASUREMENTS
6 ½ (9, 10, 11)" Foot length from back of heel

YARN
Cascade Yarns Greenland (100% merino superwash; 137 yards / 100 grams): 1 (2, 2, 2) balls #3539 Straw (A-Helen's Version) or #3518 Blue Hawaii (B-Wendy's Version)

NEEDLES
One pair straight needles size US 8 (5 mm)

One set of four double-pointed needles (dpn) size US 8 (5 mm)

Change needle size if necessary to obtain correct gauge.

NOTIONS
Stitch marker; pom pom maker (optional)

GAUGE
Helen's Version: 34 sts and 32 rows = 4" (10 cm) in Garter stitch (knit every row)

Wendy's Version: 20 sts and 24 rows = 4" (10 cm) in Bamboo stitch

HELEN'S VERSION STITCH PATTERN

1x1 Rib (multiple of 2 sts; 1-rnd repeat)

All Rnds: *K1, p1; repeat from * to end.

FOOT

Using A, CO 30 (38, 40, 40) sts, leaving 10" tail. Begin Garter st (knit every row); work even until piece measures 3 ¾ (5 ½, 6, 6 ½)" from the beginning.

(RS) Transfer sts to 3 dpns. Knit to end. Join for working in rnd; place marker (pm) for beginning of rnd.

Next Rnd: Change to 1x1 Rib; work even until piece measures 5 ½ (8, 9, 10)" from the beginning, or to 1" less than desired Foot length, end 1 st before marker; reposition marker to before last st.

TOE

Shape Toe
Next Rnd: *K2tog; repeat from * to end—15 (19, 20, 20) sts remain. Knit 1 rnd.

Next Rnd: *K2tog; repeat from * to last 1 (1, 0, 0) st(s), k1 (1, 0, 0)—8 (10, 10, 10) sts remain. Thread tail through remaining sts, pull tight, and fasten off.

FINISHING

Using CO tail, sew heel seam. Make pom-pom (see page 140, or use pom-pom maker). Tie pom pom to Slipper (see photo).

WENDY'S VERSION
STITCH PATTERNS

Bamboo Stitch (even number of sts; 2-row repeat)

Row 1 (RS): K1, *yo, k2, pass yo over last 2 sts worked; repeat from * to last st, k1.

Row 2: Purl.

Repeat Rows 1 and 2 for Bamboo Stitch.

Hourglass Rib (multiple of 4 sts; 4-rnd repeat)

Rnd 1: *K2, p2; repeat from * to end.

Rnd 2: *K2tog-tbl but do not drop sts from left-hand needle, k2tog the same sts, slipping both sts from left-hand needle together, p2; repeat from * to end.

Rnd 3: *K1, yo, k1, p2; repeat from * to end.

Rnd 4: *Skp, k1, p2; repeat from * to end.

Repeat Rnds 1-4 for Hourglass Rib.

FOOT

CO 28 (36, 40, 40) sts, leaving 10" tail. Knit 1 row. Purl 1 row. Begin Bamboo Stitch; work even until piece measures 3 ¾ (5 ½, 6, 6 ½)" from the beginning, ending with a RS row.

Next Rnd: Transfer sts to 3 dpns. Join for working in the rnd; place marker (pm) for beginning of rnd. Change to Hourglass Rib; work even until piece measures 5 ½ (8, 9, 10)" from the beginning, or to 1" less than desired Foot length, ending with Rnd 4 of pattern.

TOE

Shape Toe
Next Rnd: *K2tog, p2tog; repeat from * to end—14 (18, 20, 20) sts remain.

Next Rnd: *K1, p1; repeat from * to last st. Remove marker. Last st will be worked together with first st of next rnd.

Next Rnd: *K2tog; repeat from * to end—7 (9, 10, 10) sts remain. Thread tail through remaining sts, pull tight, and fasten off.

FLOWERS

Inner Flower
Using B, CO 36 sts. *K1, BO 4 sts; repeat from * to end—12 sts remain. Cut yarn. Thread tail through remaining sts, pull tight, and fasten off.

Outer Flower
Using B, CO 70 sts. *K1, BO 5 sts; repeat from * to end—20 sts remain. Cut yarn. Thread tail through remaining sts, pull tight, and fasten off.

FINISHING

Using CO tail, sew heel seam. Place Inner Flower over Outer Flower and tack together, then sew to Slipper.

CHICKADEE COWL

BY PAM ALLEN

Pam Allen's grandmother Bertha showed Pam how special fabric can infuse memories into quilts. This cabled cowl is similarly infused with history. It is worked in a yarn called Chickadee, spun at a historic mill in Biddeford, Maine.

FINISHED MEASUREMENTS

29" circumference x 12¾" long

YARN

Quince & Co. Chickadee (100% American wool; 181 yards / 50 grams): 4 hanks #127 Cypress

NEEDLES

One 29" (70 cm) long circular (circ) needle size US 5 (3.75 mm)

One 29" (70 cm) long circular needle size US 6 (4 mm)

Change needle size if necessary to obtain correct gauge.

NOTIONS

Cable needle (cn)

GAUGE

42 sts and 50 rnds = 5¼" (13.5 cm) in pattern from Chart A, blocked

STITCH PATTERN

1x1 Rib (multiple of 2 sts; 1-rnd repeat)

All Rnds: *K1, p1; repeat from * to end.

COWL

Using smaller needle and Long-Tail CO (see Special Techniques, page 139), CO 234 sts. Join for working in the rnd, being careful not to twist sts; pm for beginning of rnd. Begin 1x1 Rib; work even for 1". Change to larger needle.

Establish Pattern: *Work Chart A over next 42 sts, Chart B over next 7 sts, Chart C over next 22 sts, then Chart B over next 7 sts; repeat from * to end. (All charts are on page 129.) Work even until piece measures 11¾" from the beginning, ending with Row 4 or 10 of Chart A.

Change to smaller needle and 1x1 Rib; work even in rib for 1". BO all sts in pattern.

FINISHING

Block as desired.

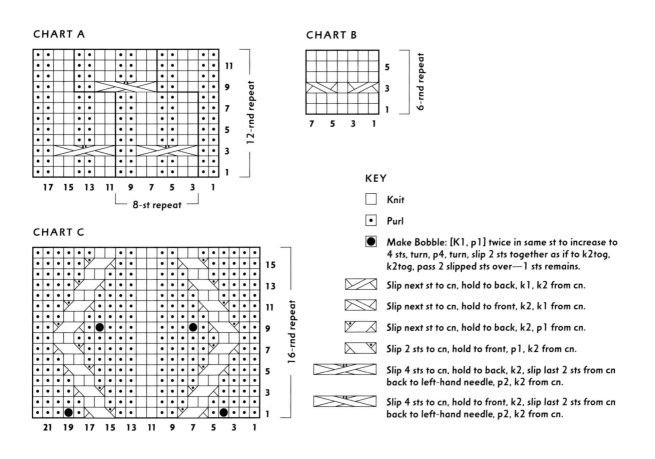

CHART A

11
9
7
5
3
1

12-rnd repeat

17 15 13 11 9 7 5 3 1

8-st repeat

CHART B

5
3
1

6-rnd repeat

7 5 3 1

CHART C

15
13
11
9
7
5
3
1

16-rnd repeat

21 19 17 15 13 11 9 7 5 3 1

KEY

☐   Knit

•   Purl

●   Make Bobble: [K1, p1] twice in same st to increase to 4 sts, turn, p4, turn, slip 2 sts together as if to k2tog, k2tog, pass 2 slipped sts over—1 sts remains.

Slip next st to cn, hold to back, k1, k2 from cn.

Slip next st to cn, hold to front, k2, k1 from cn.

Slip next st to cn, hold to back, k2, p1 from cn.

Slip 2 sts to cn, hold to front, p1, k2 from cn.

Slip 4 sts to cn, hold to back, k2, slip last 2 sts from cn back to left-hand needle, p2, k2 from cn.

Slip 4 sts to cn, hold to front, k2, slip last 2 sts from cn back to left-hand needle, p2, k2 from cn.

WAN JAI SOCKS

BY COOKIE A.

Cookie A.'s family, originally from Thailand, has migrated throughout Asia and the United States. The curved lines on these socks represent their journeys. The socks are named after Cookie's grandmother, Wan Jai, whose name translates to "sweet heart" in English.

FINISHED MEASUREMENTS

9 ½" Foot length from back of Heel

7 ½" Foot circumference

9 ½" Leg length from base of Heel

YARN

Zen Yarn Garden Serenity 20 (70% superwash merino wool / 20% cashmere / 10% nylon; 400 yards / 100 grams): 1 hank Bronzed

NEEDLES

One set of five double-pointed needles (dpn) size 1 ½ (2.5 mm)

Change needle size if necessary to obtain correct gauge.

NOTIONS

Stitch marker; cable needle (cn)

GAUGE

32 sts and 48 rnds = 4" (10 cm) in Stockinette stitch (St st)

33 sts and 48 rnds = 4" (10 cm) in cable pattern from Foot Chart

STITCH PATTERN

Twisted Rib (multiple of 11 sts; 1-rnd repeat)

All Rnds: [K1-tbl, p1] 3 times, [k1-tbl] twice, *p1, [k1-tbl, p1] 4 times, [k1-tbl] twice; repeat from * to last 3 sts, p1, k1-tbl, p1.

CUFF

CO 66 sts. Divide sts among 4 needles [16-15-17-18]. Join for working in the rnd, being careful not to twist sts; pm for beginning of rnd. Begin Twisted Rib; work even for 1 ½".

LEG

Next Rnd: Change to Leg Chart; *work Rnds 1-20, removing marker on last rnd. K3, pm for new beginning of rnd. Work Rnds 21-40, ending 3 sts before marker on last rnd, reposition marker for new beginning of rnd. Repeat from * once.

HEEL FLAP

Leave next 31 sts on hold for instep. Turn.

Row 1 (WS): Working only on 35 Heel Flap sts, *slip 1, p34, turn.

Row 2: *Slip 1, k1; repeat from * to last st, k1.

Repeat Rows 1 and 2 until Heel Flap measures 2 ¼", ending with a WS row.

TURN HEEL

Set-Up Row 1 (RS): Slip 1, k19, ssk, k1, turn.

Set-Up Row 2: Slip 1, p6, p2tog, p1, turn.

Row 1: Slip 1, knit to 1 st before gap, ssk (the 2 sts on either side of gap), k1, turn.

Row 2: Slip 1, purl to 1 st before gap, p2tog (the 2 sts on either side of gap), p1, turn.

Repeat Rows 1 and 2 five times—21 sts remain.

GUSSET

Next Row (RS): Needle 1: Slip 1, knit across Heel Flap sts, pick up and knit 1 st for each slipped st along edge of Heel Flap, pick up and knit 1 st between Heel Flap and sts on hold for Instep; **Needles 2 and 3:** Work Foot Chart across next 31 sts; **Needle 4:** Pick up and knit 1 st between Needle 3 and Heel Flap sts, pick up and knit 1 st for each slipped st along edge of Heel Flap, making sure to pick up same number of sts as for opposite side, k10 from Needle 1. Join for working in the rnd; pm for beginning of rnd.

Decrease Rnd: Needle 1: Knit to last 2 sts, k2tog; **Needles 2 and 3:** Work even as established; **Needle 4:** Ssk, knit to end—2 sts decreased. Work even for 1 rnd.

Repeat Decrease Rnd every other rnd until 66 sts remain [17-16-15-18].

FOOT

Work even until Foot measures 7 ½", or to 2" less than desired length from back of Heel.

TOE

Transfer 2 sts from Needle 4 to Needle 3 [17-16-17-16].

Next Rnd: Needle 1: Knit to last 3 sts, k2tog, k1; **Needle 2:** K1, ssk, knit to end; **Needle 3:** Knit to last 3 sts, k2tog, k1; **Needle 4:** K1, ssk, knit to end—62 sts. Knit 1 rnd.

Repeat Decrease Rnd every other rnd 9 times—26 sts remain.

FINISHING

Cut yarn, leaving long tail. Transfer sts from Needle 1 to Needle 4, and sts from Needle 3 to Needle 2. Using Kitchener st (see Special Techniques, page 000), graft Toe sts. Block as desired.

LEG CHART   **FOOT CHART**

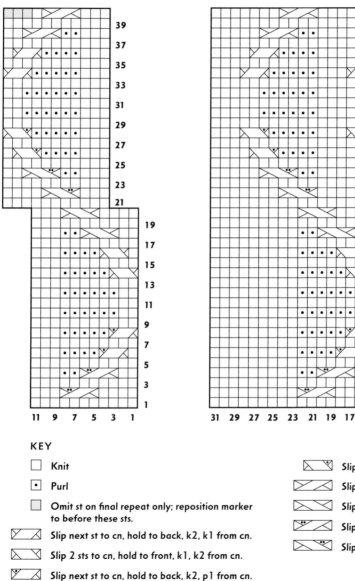

KEY

☐	Knit
⊡	Purl
▨	Omit st on final repeat only; reposition marker to before these sts.

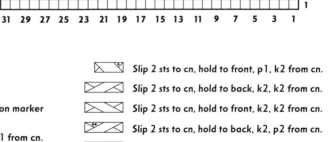

Slip next st to cn, hold to back, k2, k1 from cn.

Slip 2 sts to cn, hold to front, k1, k2 from cn.

Slip next st to cn, hold to back, k2, p1 from cn.

Slip 2 sts to cn, hold to front, p1, k2 from cn.

Slip 2 sts to cn, hold to back, k2, k2 from cn.

Slip 2 sts to cn, hold to front, k2, k2 from cn.

Slip 2 sts to cn, hold to back, k2, p2 from cn.

Slip 2 sts to cn, hold to front, p2, k2 from cn.

STORM CLOUD SHAWLETTE

BY HANNA BREETZ

This airy little shawl builds on one of the universal truths taught to knitters by Elizabeth Zimmermann—that "a circle will double its circumference in infinitely themselves-doubling distances." An elegantly simple pattern, it's easy enough for a beginner to follow and intriguing enough for a more advanced knitter to enjoy. Hanna says the way it swirls around the shoulders reminds her of misty mornings and magnificent thunderstorms.

SIZES

Small (Medium)

Note: The Small version (not shown) has no ruffle; the Medium version (shown here) has a ruffle. If desired, ruffle can be made longer; additional yarn may be required.

FINISHED MEASUREMENTS

36 (41)" wide x 14 (16)" long, before blocking

YARN

Blue Moon Fiber Arts Socks That Rock® Lightweight (100% superwash merino; 360 yards / 127 grams): 1 hank Spinel

NEEDLES

One 32" (80 cm) long or longer circular (circ) needle size US 8 (5.0 mm) circular needle

Change needle size if necessary to obtain correct gauge.

GAUGE

18 sts and 24 rows = 4" (10 cm) in pattern

Note: Gauge is not essential for this project.

SHAWLETTE

CO 4 sts.

Rows 1, 3, 5, 7, and 9 (RS): K1, *yo, k1; repeat from * to end.

Rows 2 and 4: Knit—13 sts after Row 4.

Rows 6 and 8: Knit, dropping all yarnovers.

Rows 10 and 11, 20 and 21, and 38 and 39: Repeat Rows 2 and 3—97 sts after Row 38.

Rows 12-19, 22-37, and 40-69: Repeat Rows 6 and 7.

Row 70: Repeat Row 6.

SIZE SMALL ONLY
BO all sts very loosely.

SIZE MEDIUM ONLY
Row 71: Repeat Row 3.

Row 72: Repeat Row 2—193 sts.

Rows 73-84: Repeat Rows 5 and 6. BO all sts loosely.

FINISHING

Block as desired.

ABBREVIATIONS

BO: Bind off

Ch: Chain

Circ: Circular

Cn: Cable needle

CO: Cast on

Dpn: Double-pointed needle(s)

K1-f/b: Knit into the front loop and back loop of the same stitch to increase 1 stitch.

K1-f/b/f: Knit into the front loop, back loop, then front loop of the same stitch to increase 2 stitches.

K1-tbl: Knit 1 stitch through the back loop.

K2tog: Knit 2 stitches together.

K3tog: Knit 3 stitches together.

K: Knit

LLI (left lifted increase): Pick up the stitch below the last stitch on the right-hand needle and place on the left-hand needle; knit the picked-up stitch through the back loop.

M1 or **M1-l** (make 1-left slanting): With the tip of the left-hand needle inserted from front to back, lift the strand between the 2 needles onto the left-hand needle; knit the strand through the back loop to increase 1 stitch.

M1-p (make 1 purlwise-right slanting): With tip of left-hand needle inserted from back to front, lift strand between 2 needles onto left-hand needle; purl strand through front loop to increase 1 stitch.

M1-r (make 1-right slanting): With tip of left-hand needle inserted from back to front, lift strand between 2 needles onto left-hand needle; knit strand through front loop to increase 1 stitch.

P1-tbl: Purl 1 stitch through the back loop.

P2tog: Purl 2 stitches together.

Pm: Place marker

P: Purl

Psso (pass slipped stitch over): Pass the slipped stitch on the right-hand needle over the stitch(es) indicated in the instructions, as in binding off.

Rnd(s): Round(s)

RLI (right lifted increase): Pick up the stitch below the next stitch on the left-hand needle and place it on the left-hand needle; knit the picked-up stitch.

RS: Right side

S2kp2: Slip the next 2 stitches together to the right-hand needle as if to knit 2 together, k1, pass the 2 slipped stitches over.

Sc (single crochet): Insert the hook into the next stitch and draw up a loop (2 loops on the hook), yarn over and draw through both loops on the hook.

Skp (slip, knit, pass): Slip the next stitch knitwise to the right-hand needle, k1, pass the slipped stitch over the knit stitch.

Sk2p (double decrease): Slip the next stitch knitwise to the right-hand needle, k2tog, pass the slipped stitch over the stitch from the k2tog.

Sm: Slip marker

Ssk (slip, slip, knit): Slip the next 2 stitches to the right-hand needle one at a time as if to knit; return them to the left-hand needle one at a time in their new orientation; knit them together through the back loops.

St(s): Stitch(es)

Tbl: Through the back loop

Tog: Together

Wrp-t: Wrap and turn (see Special Techniques—Short Row Shaping)

WS: Wrong side

Yo: Yarnover (see Special Techniques)

Yrn: Yarn round needle

SPECIAL TECHNIQUES

Backward Loop CO: Make a loop (using a slip knot) with the working yarn and place it on the right-hand needle (first st CO), * wind yarn around thumb clockwise, insert right-hand needle into the front of the loop on thumb, remove thumb and tighten st on needle; repeat from * for remaining sts to be CO, or for casting on at the end of a row in progress.

Cable CO: Make a loop (using a slip knot) with the working yarn and place it on the left-hand needle (first st CO), knit into slip knot, draw up a loop but do not drop st from left-hand needle; place new loop on left-hand needle; * insert the tip of the right-hand needle into the space between the last 2 sts on the left-hand needle and draw up a loop; place the loop on the left-hand needle. Repeat from * for remaining sts to be CO, or for casting on at the end of a row in progress.

Duplicate Stitch: Duplicate st is similar to Kitchener st, except it is used for decorative purposes instead of joining two pieces together. Thread a tapestry needle with chosen yarn and leaving a tail to be woven in later, * bring the needle from WS to RS of work at the base of the st to be covered, pass the needle under both loops (the base of the st above) above the st to be covered; insert the needle into same place where you started (base of st), and pull yarn through to WS of work. Be sure that the new st is the same tension as the rest of the piece. Repeat from * for additional sts.

A good way to visualize the path of the yarn for Duplicate st is to work a swatch in Stockinette st using main color (MC) for three rows, work 1 row alternating one stitch in MC and one stitch in contrasting color (CC), then work two additional rows using MC only.

I-Cord: Using a double-pointed needle, cast on or pick up the required number of sts; the working yarn will be at the left-hand side of the needle. * Transfer the needle with the sts to your left hand, bring the yarn around behind the work to the right-hand side; using a second double-pointed needle, knit the sts from right to left, pulling the yarn from left to right for the first st; do not turn. Slide the sts to the opposite end of the needle; repeat from * until the I-Cord is the length desired. *Note: After a few rows, the tubular shape will become apparent.*

Judy's Magic CO: *Make a slipknot and place it on one of two needles; the slipknot will count as the first cast-on stitch. Hold the two needles together in your right hand, with the slipknot on the top needle (Needle 2), the tail yarn coming from the top needle and over your left index finger, and the working yarn coming from under the bottom needle (Needle 1) and over your left thumb (this is the opposite of how you hold the yarns for Long-Tail CO—see below). * Bring the tip of Needle 1 over the top of the tail yarn, then back under the tail to the front, so that the yarn is now in between the needles, and you have one stitch cast onto Needle 1. * Bring the tip of Needle 2 in front of the working yarn, then underneath the yarn from front to back, slipping the yarn in between the needles, so that you have two stitches cast onto Needle 2 (including the slipknot). Repeat from * to * until you have the required number of sts on your needles. When you work the first stitch of the first round with the working yarn, make sure that the tail lies under the working yarn. The first stitch may loosen as you work the round; to tighten it up, gently pull on the yarn tail. See www.persistentillusion.com for photos and links to videos of this cast-on technique.*

Kitchener Stitch: *Using a blunt tapestry needle, thread a length of yarn approximately 4 times the length of the section to be joined. Hold the pieces to be joined wrong sides together, with the needles holding the sts parallel, both ends pointing to the right. Working from right to left, insert tapestry needle into first st on front needle as if to purl, pull yarn through, leaving st on needle; insert tapestry needle into first st on back needle as if to knit, pull yarn through, leaving st on needle; * insert tapestry needle into first st on front needle as if to knit, pull yarn through, remove st from needle; insert tapestry needle into next st on front needle as if to purl, pull yarn through, leave st on needle; insert tapestry needle into first st on back needle as if to purl, pull yarn through, remove st from needle; insert tapestry needle into next st on back needle as if to knit, pull yarn through, leave st on needle. Repeat from *, working 3 or 4 sts at a time, then go back and adjust tension to match the pieces being joined. When 1 st remains on each needle, cut yarn and pass through last 2 sts to fasten off.*

Long-Tail (Thumb) CO: *Leaving tail with about 1" of yarn for each st to be cast-on, make a slipknot in the yarn and place it on the right-hand needle, with the tail to the front and the working end to the back. Insert the thumb and forefinger of left hand between the strands of yarn so the working end is around forefinger, and the tail end is around thumb "slingshot" fashion; * insert the tip of the right-hand needle into the front loop on the thumb, hook the strand of yarn coming from the forefinger from back to front, and draw it through the loop on thumb; remove thumb from the loop and pull on the working yarn to tighten the new st on the right-hand needle; return thumb and forefinger to their original positions, and repeat from * for remaining sts to be CO.*

Pom-Pom: Use a pom-pom maker or the following method: Holding middle and forefingers close together, but not touching, wrap yarn around both fingers 50 or more times (enough to make a thick pom-pom), making sure not to wrap yarn too tightly. *Note: Holding fingers close together will result in approximately 1" pom-poms; holding them farther apart will result in larger pom-poms.* Cut yarn. Cut additional strand of yarn 12" long for tie. Thread one end of tie between fingers, closer to palm, and the other end between finger-tips, making sure this strand passes around the outside of all the wrapped pom-pom strands. Tie a single knot as tightly as possible, then slide the wrapped pom-pom off the fingers and tighten the knot, adding a second knot to secure. Cut through all the looped ends. Fluff the pom-pom strands until you have a ball. Trim the ends so that the ball is even all around, making sure not to trim the tie strands. Using ends of tie, sew pom-pom to garment.

Reading Charts: Unless otherwise specified in the instructions, when working straight, charts are read from right to left for RS rows, from left to right for WS rows. Row numbers are written at the beginning of each row. Numbers on the right indicate RS rows; numbers on the left indicate WS rows. When working circular, all rounds are read from right to left.

Short Row Shaping: Work the number of sts specified in the instructions, wrap and turn (wrp-t) as follows:

To wrap a knit st, bring yarn to the front (purl position), slip the next st purlwise to the right-hand needle, bring yarn to the back of work, return the slipped st on the right-hand needle to the left-hand needle purlwise; turn, ready to work the next row, leaving the remaining sts unworked. To wrap a purl stitch, work as for wrapping a knit st, but bring yarn to the back (knit position) before slipping the stitch, and to the front after slipping the stitch.

When short rows are completed, or when working progressively longer short rows, work the wrap together with the wrapped st as you come to it as follows:

If st is to be worked as a knit st, insert the right-hand needle into the wrap, from below, then into the wrapped st; k2tog; if st to be worked is a purl st, insert needle into the wrapped st, then down into the wrap; p2tog. (Wrap may be lifted onto the left-hand needle, then worked together with the wrapped st if this is easier.)

Stranded (Fair Isle) Colorwork Method: When more than one color is used per row, carry color(s) not in use loosely across the WS of work. Be sure to secure all colors at beginning and end of rows to prevent holes.

Yarn over (yo) other than beginning of row: Bring yarn forward (to the purl position), then place it in position to work the next st. If next st is to be knit, bring yarn over the needle and knit; if next st is to be purled, bring yarn over the needle and then forward again to the purl position and purl. Work the yarnover in pattern on the next row unless instructed otherwise.

RESOURCES

SOURCES FOR SUPPLIES

Berroco
berroco.com

Blue Moon Fiber Arts
bluemoonfiberarts.com

Cascade Yarns
cascadeyarns.com

Jamieson's of Shetland
jamiesonsshetland.co.uk

Lantern Moon
(provided some of the buttons for this book)
lanternmoon.com

Manos del Uruguay
fairmountfibers.com
artesanoyarns.co.uk

Pico Accuardi Dyeworks
picoaccuardi.com

Quince & Co.
quinceandco.com

Rowan
knitrowan.com

St-Denis Yarns
stdenisyarns.com

Shibui Knits
shibuiknits.com

Tahki Stacy Charles, Inc.
(distributor of Loop-d-Loop by Teva Durham)
tahkistacycharles.com

Zen Yarn Garden
zenyarngarden.com

DESIGNER WEBSITES AND BLOGS

Pam Allen
quinceandco.com

Judy Becker
persistentillusion.com

Wendy Bernard
knitandtonic.net

Adrian Bizilia
helloyarn.com

Hanna Breetz
evergreenknits.blogspot.com

Larissa Brown
stitchmarker.net

David Castillo
gogodavitron.com

Cookie A.
cookiea.com

Cosette Cornelius-Bates
cosymates.com

Teva Durham
loop-d-loop.com

Jared Flood
brooklyntweed.net

Chrissy Gardiner
gardineryarnworks.com

Kay Gardiner
masondixonknitting.com

Norah Gaughan
berroco.com

Anne Hanson
knitspot.com

Emily Johnson
familytrunkproject.com

Kirsten Kapur
throughtheloops.typepad.com

Jessica Marshall Forbes
ravelry.com

Joan McGowan-Michael
whiteliesdesigns.com

Robin Melanson
robinmelanson.com

Leigh Radford
leighradford.com

Cirilia Rose
ravelry.com/designers/cirilia-rose

Kristin Spurkland
heitherekrissy.typepad.com/blog

Meg Swansen
schoolhousepress.com

Ysolda Teague
ysolda.com

THANK YOU

Thank you to all the knitters and designers who shared their stories with me.

To sample knitters: Francine Matagrano Ferrara, Christy Pagels, Evelyn Silverman, Maria Rose, Stevanie Pico, Sue Green, Melinda Goodwin, Diana McIntosh, Hannah Cuviello, Gwen Schnurman, and Cathy Woodcock. To models: Jane Van Lom, Sally Woodcock, Hau Hagedorn, Olivia Fitzpatrick and her grandpa Mike, David Dunbabin and his mother Shannon, Elizabeth Courtenay Grace Waldorf, Zachary Waldorf, Sebastian Brown, and Eileen Golden. To those who contributed to the photo shoot: Monticello Antiques Marketplace, Lantern Moon, Tina Tam, and my neighbor Dave. Styling is by Stevanie Pico. To my sister Lynette Golden Fitzpatrick, for her photography of Nanny's blanket on page 9.

To the team who made this book: Melanie Falick, Betty Christiansen, Anna Christian, Michael Crouser, Sue McCain, and Scott Mendel.

To friends and family: Martin John Brown, Sebastian Brown, Eileen Golden, the Picos, Jonny Waldorf, Peg Hamilton, Deb Accuardi, Shannon Dunbabin, Amy Jones, Holly Hammershoy, and a special thanks to Cascade Yarns.

The author and her grandmother, Olive, around 1975.

LARISSA BROWN began knitting when she was five years old, hanging out on her grandmother Olive's chenille couch in her suburban New Jersey home. Today she lives in Portland, Oregon, where she designs knitting patterns and dyes yarn with Pico Accuardi Dyeworks. In 2008, together with her husband, Martin John Brown, she wrote the book *Knitalong: Celebrating the Tradition of Knitting Together*. See her work at StitchMarker.net.

PUBLISHED IN 2011 BY STEWART, TABORI & CHANG
AN IMPRINT OF ABRAMS

Text copyright © 2011 Larissa Brown
Photographs copyright © 2011 Michael Crouser (unless otherwise noted)
Note: All family photos belong to designers profiled.

Library of Congress Cataloging-in-Publication Data:
Brown, Larissa Golden, 1968-
My grandmother's knitting / by Larissa Brown.
p. cm.
"A Melanie Falick book."
ISBN 978-1-58479-939-9 (alk. paper)
1. Knitting. 2. Knitters (Persons) I. Title.
TT820.B833 2011
746.43'2—dc22   2010052319

EDITOR: MELANIE FALICK
DESIGNER: ANNA CHRISTIAN
PRODUCTION MANAGER: TINA CAMERON

The text of this book was composed in Arta and Vendetta.

Printed and bound in China

10 9 8 7 6 5 4 3 2 1

THE ART OF BOOKS SINCE 1949

115 WEST 18TH STREET
NEW YORK, NY 10011
WWW.ABRAMSBOOKS.COM